KINDLE MY HEART

VOLUME I

WISDOM AND INSPIRATION FROM A LIVING MASTER

GURUMAYI CHIDVILASANANDA

PRENTICE
HALL
PRESS

New York   London   Toronto   Sydney   Tokyo   Singapore

ACKNOWLEDGMENTS

Our grateful appreciation goes to Cynthia Kline, George Franklin, Jane Ferrar,
Charity James, and Joseph Chilton Pearce, who helped in the selection and
editing of the talks, to Shane Conroy for his design and embossed illustration,
to Christian Kaviiik Gavignet for his cover and text illustrations,
to Ed Levy for copyediting the text, to Leesa Stanion for compiling the index,
to Steve Batliner and Adriana de la Torre for typesetting,
and to Frances Aitken, Pat Arnsfield, Peggy Bendet, Claire James,
and Lalita Lopez, who helped prepare the manuscript for publication.

Swami Kripananda

Excerpts reprinted from *The Prophet*, by Kahlil Gibran, by permission of
Alfred A. Knopf, Inc. Copyright 1923 by Kahlil Gibran and renewed 1951 by
Administrators C.T.A. of the Kahlil Gibran Estate and Mary G. Gibran.

NOTE ON THE USE OF SANSKRIT

All Sanskrit words are italicized the first time they appear in each chapter.
The long vowels, "ā," ī," and "ū," are marked with a diacritical
above the character, and are held twice as long as the short vowels, "a," "i,"
and "u." The appearance of "ñ" signifies a *nya* sound, similar to
the *ni* in the English word "*onion*." After the first usage in each chapter,
Sanskrit words are set in roman type without diacritical marks.
Sanskrit words not defined in context and other unfamiliar
terms are defined in the Glossary.

PRENTICE HALL PRESS
15 Columbus Circle
New York, NY 10023

Copyright © 1989 by SYDA Foundation

(Swami) MUKTANANDA, (Swami) CHIDVILASANANDA, GURUMAYI,
SHAKTIPAT, SIDDHA MEDITATION and SIDDHA YOGA
are registered service marks of SYDA Foundation in the U.S.A.
and may be registered in other countries.

PRENTICE HALL PRESS and colophons are registered trademarks
of Simon & Schuster, Inc.

Library of Congress Catalog Card Number: 90-52647

ISBN 0-13-515347-6

Manufactured in the United States of America

10 9 8 7 6 5 4 3 2 1

First Prentice Hall Press Edition

CONTENTS

VOLUME I

A LIVING MASTER

FROM THE TIME OF THE ANCIENT SAGES, the power of the Siddhas has passed from Guru to disciple, linking Master to Master in an unbroken chain of grace. Gurumayi Chidvilasananda is the living Guru of the Siddha tradition. Through Shaktipat initiation, she awakens the Kundalini energy in a seeker and guides the course of the divine energy as it illumines the higher realms of awareness. Her own Master, Baba Muktananda, prepared her from early childhood to fulfill this extraordinary destiny, having himself received the power of the Siddha lineage from his Guru, Bhagawan Nityananda, a revered saint of India.

Gurumayi bestows grace upon all who come into her presence. She lives in a state which transcends the barriers of limited individuality, and from this state she guides the seeker on the path of union between the individual soul and the universal Soul.

Gurumayi first met her Guru when she was five years old. At that moment, there was a mystical outpouring of love and recognition, a classic meeting between a true Guru and a true disciple. From that time on, she felt that her life belonged to him. Nine years later Baba gave her Shaktipat. With the awakening of the inner energy, her life became an offering on the altar of service and divine love. As he prepared her to receive the full power of the lineage, she experienced with greater and greater intensity the profound mysteries of the unfolding inner universe.

Always she was the perfect disciple, absorbing herself in his state. At his command, she completed her formal education. Then, as he journeyed around the world, she was at his side, translating for him and serving him with one-pointed attention. Following the path of supreme devotion to Guru, God, and Self, she attained the state of Realization.

Shortly before Baba Muktananda left his body in October 1982, he commanded Gurumayi to succeed him, and transferred to her the grace-bestowing power of the lineage. Honoring that command, she gives to all who turn to her a direct experience of the timeless message of the Siddhas: "Meditate on your Self, worship your Self, honor your Self. Your God dwells within you as you."

NOTE TO THE READER

EVERY LIVING CREATURE is drawn to the light of divine love, for in its warmth are laughter, contentment, knowledge, and union. Often the inner voice of the heart calls out with yearning for the experience of its own perfect love. Praying for the awakening of this inner love, a devotee sings:

> Kindle my heart's flame with thy flame,
> O Guru, kindle my heart's flame with thine.
> Remove the darkness covering my heart,
> Shower the nectar of love upon us.
> Awaken us!

Just as a candle can be lit from a fire, so the spark of love and knowledge within us can be kindled by contact with one whose flame of love is fully ablaze. This is why, out of their great compassion, saints and sages give their lives to others so that what they have received may in turn be given.

Kindle My Heart is a selection of talks given by Gurumayi Chidvilas-ananda as she traveled around the world in 1985 and 1986. Her journey, which started in India, took her to Japan, Hawaii, California, Mexico, Florida, Georgia, New York, New England, once again to New York, on to London, and finally back to India.

In her talks, Gurumayi does not speak "about" a subject — her thoughts, words, and actions are one. Her inner experience is not different from her words. She is what she speaks about. Just as the words are not ordinary, so the reading of them need not be ordinary. These talks are meant for us personally. They are not philosophies or ideas to be learned or studied. If we are open to them, they will enter us directly and kindle the flame of our hearts. The power of the words of a great being draws us into states of stillness, contemplation, and meditation. Reading with our hearts in this way, we receive what is being offered.

One look, one word, one thought, one touch of a saint can change our lives forever. Thousands of people who came to meet Gurumayi during her tour had a direct experience of this. Each night she spoke on a different theme, and she would sing the ecstatic poetry of the saints, drawing all who heard her closer to the voice of their own inner being.

Gurumayi quotes from the scriptures in every talk. Although she cites the holy books of all traditions, the philosophies of Vedanta and Kashmir Shaivism are those which most closely approximate her own direct experience. Without the experience there is intellectual knowledge but no ecstasy — understanding but no love. With the experience, knowledge and ecstasy merge.

As we read these talks, we are in the presence of an enlightened Master, and we feel the power of love, the power of the Truth. We begin to see ourselves clearly; and we can laugh at the play of our own minds, which she describes with so much compassion and humor. Our attention is drawn inward, and as she takes us into meditation with the mantra of her lineage, *Om Namah Shivāya*, we begin to feel the words and the experience behind the words merge. In this way, the flame of the heart is mysteriously kindled.

At the end of her tour, Gurumayi said, "For me, this whole tour has been the presence of my Guru, Baba Muktananda. Through his grace, Baba has made it possible for us to go from place to place, making each stop a home. All the people in each place are much closer than one's own Self. Meeting you all, I feel you are dearer than anything else in this world. All this can happen only through Baba's grace and through Baba's will and through Baba's love."

The Editors

FOREWORD

THE WORLD OF SHOW BUSINESS promises fame, adulation, success, and money. Having attained all these (for which I am very grateful) I have nevertheless come to realize that they *alone* do not bring you true happiness. True happiness comes from within. Understanding this is one thing; experiencing it is something else!

In September 1985, I met Gurumayi Chidvilasananda — a spiritual Master whose life is dedicated to helping people attain this experience. The encounter took place at Heathrow Airport. Gurumayi was flying to India, and her European devotees eagerly took the opportunity to arrange a meeting with her while her plane was refueling in London.

So there I was with eight hundred strangers at seven in the morning, and what I experienced was so powerful that had I not been there I could scarcely have believed it possible. A feeling of absolute and indescribable bliss swept over me, and tears of joy ran down my cheeks. From that moment, meditation, which I had been trying to practice unsuccessfully for some time, suddenly became very easy. Since then I am often able to recall that initial experience during meditation, and it always helps me to focus on what is really important in my life.

Walking the spiritual path — something we all need to do so desperately in these mixed-up times — is by no means an easy task. But with a great Siddha teacher like Gurumayi to guide us with such divine love, it is quite remarkable how one progresses. I used to feel that my working life and my family life were pulling me in different directions. Since meeting Gurumayi, I know there are no divisions at all in my life.

Lulu, London, April 1988

INTRODUCTION

THE GREAT POET-SAINT JNANESHWAR MAHARAJ says: "If your heart, through merit, should be illumined even a little by the wisdom of one who is a knower of the Truth, then every fear of life in this world would be removed." But how do we come to meet a "knower of the Truth"? And what does it mean to have your heart illumined?

There were always two books on the polished oak dresser in my father's bedroom. Nothing was ever said about them, except that they were about yoga, and that they had been given to him by a friend who was stationed in Kashmir during the war. I used to look up at those books and wonder. I sensed they were important, but I never actually read them, thinking they would be too difficult to understand. Years later, studying philosophy at university, I had the same experience of coming close to some knowledge of the Truth but not being able to take hold of it, until one evening my tutorial group discussed the life of the nineteenth-century saint Ramakrishna Paramahamsa. As we spoke, the room filled with peace and a sense of well-being, and I suddenly felt the presence of something deeply familiar and deeply loved. Contemplating the life of a saint, I felt I had found what I had always looked for, some quality that tied together all my hopes for a beautiful life.

As this contemplation continued, it took me into another world. I started to have dreams of a large dark man with an extraordinarily charismatic and mysterious energy, who invited me to join a troupe he was training in an esoteric sword dance. I saw myself moving about inside a light, and when I walked it was as if I was traveling over the earth toward some definite destination. I felt pulled and pulled to go to India, to see if any saints were living there now.

One day I set off on that very unlikely journey. I left England on a foggy September morning, traveled by car through Europe and the Middle East as far as Teheran, and went on from there by bus and train. I had thought it would be arduous and perhaps dangerous to travel such a long way into unknown territory, and I expected the trip to take at least two to three months. Less than three weeks later I crossed the border into India, stunned by a journey that had been one of the most remarkable experiences of my life. It had been neither arduous nor dangerous; it had just been a continuation of that same sensation of riding inside an area of light that seemed to be moving in a certain direction, at a certain steady speed. I had been totally protected, not only from danger, but also from any sideshow that might have distracted me from the goal of my pilgrimage.

I soon found myself in the city of Bombay, having lunch with a woman I had just met and her entire family, listening to them tell me stories of a living saint, Baba Muktananda, whom they visited regularly. In fact, they were planning to go to his *āshram* the next day. Would I be interested in going along?

Baba Muktananda was not at the ashram when we arrived. He would be returning in a few days, we were told, from a four-month tour of the West. So I waited. And then, early one morning, there he was, standing under the arch of the front gate, quiet and still, with the roar of the welcoming crowds, cymbals clashing, and conches blaring all around him.

In the days that followed, he appeared to grow and grow; he seemed to become younger, more regal, more vibrant by the hour. I was somewhat perplexed and more than a little overwhelmed. Could he really be over sixty? Why did he seem like a king? Why was he so strong and so happy and beautiful? Yet something inside me recognized and responded to Baba immediately as "the Truth."

When I was introduced, he welcomed me by saying, "You can continue your studies in my library." The last place in the world I wanted to be at that moment was back in an academic niche; I had hoped I was ready for a different kind of experience. But the Master had spoken. So I trudged up the stairs to investigate the library. The door was locked. No hours were posted either, just a sign which read: All Knowledge is Worthless Compared to the Knowledge of the Guru's Feet. I went happily back down the stairs and off to work in the garden. Life with the Guru had begun.

One evening, after I had been in the ashram for several weeks, Baba called me to his seat in the courtyard and gave me a *mala*, a string of *japa* beads he had been twirling around his fingers. Thrilled that he would give me a gift — and such a gift! — I headed straight for my room, locked the door, lit a candle before the picture of the Guru, and sat down to repeat the mantra. But instead of *Om Namah Shivāya*, the words of the prayer *Jyota se Jyota* started repeating inside me, "Kindle my heart's flame with thy flame. O Guru, kindle my heart's flame with thine."

This prayer, sung every day in the ashram, had not until then made a particularly deep impression on me. Yet, at that moment, as it spontaneously welled up and sang itself in my heart, I felt the impact of each word. I felt my whole being was inside my heart, but it was a heart I had never known before. I had lived up to that moment with no idea that such love existed inside me. As the verses of the prayer came to an end, I heard the name "Gurudev, Gurudev" repeating and repeating. It seemed to be Baba's name and the name of this love: the Guru *was* this love. Nothing else in life could come close to it. It was a love all by itself, a light apart.

As time went by, I realized that the Guru was the guiding light that had surrounded me and brought me safely to Baba. Only the living Guru could show me that I, too, was that light, I was that love. Over and over, that light would push me toward Baba — and Baba would push me toward that light. I cannot say my love for him increased bit by bit. It was instead as if the immense love for the Guru which was already there, as a natural state, became more and more apparent to me; and as it was uncovered, my life became more and more my own.

When Baba Muktananda died in 1982, the Ganeshpuri Ashram seemed to be suspended in a timeless, deathless present. It did not feel like death at all. Wave upon wave of love tied everyone together and held us close. Love proved to be stronger than grief, and that was a very real testimony to what Baba's life had been. Then the real miracle began to take place.

"She is a great flame," Baba said of Gurumayi when she was still a young girl. "One day she will illumine the world." And now the presence, the love, the light that had been Baba resided in Gurumayi. The transfer of power was mysterious and entire. Although it affected both the surface and substance of daily life, it transpired most power-fully on the inside. It was invisible yet palpable, and awesome to behold. Gurumayi took her seat as the Guru, the radiant vehicle of the Shakti, the personification of love on the outside and the flame of love in our hearts. Looking at Gurumayi in the days and weeks following Baba's *mahāsamadhi*, I understood, in a way I had never dared imagine, that what he had always said was true: the Guru is not the body, the Guru is the grace-bestowing power of God, the Shakti, the inner light.

In 1986, I was asked to help prepare this collection of Gurumayi's talks for publication. As soon as the work began, it changed the lives of everyone involved. It was a deep, transforming delight to live in the Guru's words every day and experience her thoughts flowing as poetry out of that place of Truth. Keeping the company of Gurumayi's talks was like being with her, like having her *darshan* continually. It did not seem to matter what else was happening — what my mood was, or where I began to read — I would be filled with her wisdom, and would have an immediate and strong experience of love, bursting out from inside and seeming to literally press on my heart, to dance in my blood.

This work provided the gift of outer darshan as well. One evening we were working late when Gurumayi appeared at the end of the corridor and began firing questions at me. As she spoke, my whole body was being lit up from inside; her words were like the beams of a searchlight, illuminating every cell. As I looked through these illuminated particles of myself, I found it easy to reply simply and truthfully. Then, when I looked at Gurumayi, I saw her surrounded by flames. It was as if she had dissolved into a column of fire. I stood there, free of fear, marveling at the sight. Then, when Gurumayi finished speaking, I discovered that I, too, was a blazing column. My body was like a pillar of fire, but there was no heat in the flames, only radiance.

The next moment, Gurumayi began to speak to other people who were standing nearby, turning the whole subject into a joke. And then she was gone around the corner, just as suddenly as she had come. What had she done? She had given me the precious gift of her darshan: fire beneath a white marble arch; grace in the form of words like lightning bolts, charging every cell in my body; energy to finish the work with inspiration and love.

Kindle My Heart, this first collection of talks by Gurumayi, has been eagerly awaited. The subject of these talks is our lives: what is and what can be, the known and the Great Unknown. Told from the perspective of the Truth, it is a book of essential knowledge about ourselves; we do not find in it anything that is foreign or difficult to understand. At the same time, the talks go beyond the range of our everyday understanding, for they are about the life that begins with the awakening of the inner energy — the awakening that happens through the grace of a spiritual Master. This initiation revolutionizes our life, putting it on an entirely different basis, and initiates a way of being that focuses on the true life of the heart.

Quoting the great *Sufi* poet Jalalu'd-Din Rumi, Gurumayi calls us to:

> Come out of the circle of time
> And into the circle of love.

The awakening by the Master releases us from the world created by the circle of Time. When we are bound by thoughts and identifications, we swing between pleasure and pain, happiness and unhappiness; we have no real life at all. In *Kindle My Heart*, Gurumayi leads us out of the house of our mundane existence into the light of our own being, into the circle of Love. She shows us that in the presence of the highest Truth, we experience love; and that Truth, that love, exists to be experienced in every moment of our lives. This is a reversal of our usual approach to life. "It is not satisfying our desires which takes us to the Highest," Gurumayi says. "On the contrary, it is by going to the Highest that we find all of our desires fulfilled." It is because they have had this experience that all the great beings say, Look within. This is where you will find the Truth. Look within. This is where you will find everything.

This book is filled with that Truth which is timeless, which applies no matter where we are, who we think we are, or what we are doing with our lives. Whether we are young or old on the spiritual path, Eastern or Western in our thinking, social or private in our concerns, whether we have a little interest in meditation or a burning desire to serve God — as we read *Kindle My Heart*, somewhere in the space between the words, our hearts catch on fire with love for God, love for the Truth, and love for life.

A true spiritual Master embodies the Truth in a completely literal sense, and so what flows from Gurumayi is only love. In her presence, we have an experience of the real nature of our being — pure awareness, light, love, and the bliss of contentment. These talks flow from that light, and they are infused with that love.

Cynthia Kline
South Fallsburg, New York
September 16, 1988

THE TALKS

Muktānandāya gurave
shishya-samsāra-hārine
Bhakta-kāryaika-dehāya
namaste chit-sad-ātmane

Om namah shivāya gurave
sac-chid-ānanda-mūrtaye
Nishprapañchāya shāntāya
nirālambāya tejase

Om saha nāvavatu
Saha nau bhunaktu
Saha vīryam karavavahai
Tejasvi nāvadhītam astu
Mā vidvishāvahai

Om shāntih shāntih shāntih
Sadgurunāth Mahārāj kī Jay!

Salutations to Muktananda, the Guru,
who rescues his disciples from the cycle of birth and death,
who has assumed a body to meet the needs of his devotees,
whose nature is Consciousness and Being.

Om. Salutations to the Guru, who is Shiva!
His form is Being, Consciousness, and Bliss.
He is transcendent, calm, free from all support,
and luminous.

Om. May we, Guru and disciple,
be protected together.
May we be nourished together.
May we achieve strength together.
May our knowledge turn into light.
May we never lose patience with one another.

Om. Peace! Peace! Peace!
I hail the Master who has revealed the Truth to me!

Contemplation of the Truth

Tokyo, December 18, 1985

WITH GREAT RESPECT AND LOVE, I welcome you all with all my heart. Swami Muktananda, our Guru, taught us to respect one another. He taught it, and he lived what he taught. Many of us hear the teaching "Respect one another," but we do not listen to it. Even if we listen to it, we do not necessarily practice it. It is amazing that we all know about this great teaching, but somehow we do not know how to incorporate it into our lives. We think we respect one another, but this respect does not show in our actions. Why?

In the *Bhagavad Gītā* the Lord says:

> Let a person uplift himself by his own Self;
> Let him not lower himself.
> The Self alone is one's friend,
> And the Self alone is one's enemy.

Although Lord Krishna says "Uplift yourself," we are not able to do that. We think we are unworthy, we think we are full of negativities and doubts, and these weigh us down. Even if we imagine we respect one another, what comes across is our low opinion of ourselves. It does not matter if we are scholars, professionals, or great businessmen; beneath our erudition and professional success we feel a lack of worth, we feel we are not what we should be.

This feeling of unworthiness creates disrespect. If we do not feel greatness or divinity in ourselves, if we do not experience the Truth within, how can we recognize that greatness and that Truth in others? This is the reason that, even though the great beings teach us to respect one another, we are not able to imbibe their teaching.

To make the Truth our own, we have to prepare the field of the body. In order to make his field flower, a farmer must first weed it, plow it, seed it, and irrigate it. But in order to ensure the flowering of wisdom in the field of the body, we cannot use a tractor or a shovel to dig it up; we must employ more subtle practices. And so we chant, we contemplate, and we meditate.

As we chant, even if we do not understand the power behind each syllable, it goes through us, and even if every one of us is not chanting, that power enters our ears and permeates our system.

When we contemplate "Who am I? Why was I born? What is the purpose of this world?" even if we do not find the answers immediately, the inquiry itself creates energy. Most of us live without ever trying to find out the cause of our being here and the cause of the universe. Of course, we study these things in school and in college, and we learn the theories that others have come up with, but we do not try to find the answers from within our own being. That is more difficult, isn't it?

How can we chant, contemplate, and meditate so as to live the life we must live? Although chanting is very sweet and beautiful, we cannot always chant aloud when we are walking down the street. So when we are together like this or when we are by ourselves, we chant to ourselves constantly. As we practice chanting, our whole being accepts the sound. Then, regardless of the situation in which we find ourselves, we hear the sound, and it protects us.

We practice contemplation. Although we are not always comfortable with what we are contemplating, we continue our inner inquiry. As we contemplate more and more, the answer reveals itself to us.

For some, the answer reveals itself as supreme contentment. No matter what their circumstances may be, such people are content. Whether there is heat or cold, honor or dishonor, praise or blame, they experience supreme contentment within.

For some, the answer comes as divine intoxication. Many people drink to feel high and to block their emotions and anxieties. But when you truly contemplate, the Truth reveals itself as divine intoxication. No matter what is happening, you experience a high state. Someone may be yelling at you, and you think, "Listen to that — the glory of God!" In everything and everyone you experience only intoxication, ecstasy.

Some people experience the answer as absolute enlightenment, complete serenity. When the Truth reveals itself to you, no matter what form it takes, it is the Truth. However, who has the patience to wait for the Truth to reveal itself? Until that revelation comes, we spend our time being jealous of other people, getting angry with them, and thinking bad thoughts about them. In Vedanta this is called *māyā*, illusion. In the beginning there was enlightenment, and at the end there will be enlightenment, but in the middle there is a drama. We do *sādhanā*, we do our practices, to avoid being totally involved in the drama of maya.

In the *Gītā* the Lord says:

> With his mind completely harmonized by yoga,
> The yogi sees the inner Self abiding in all beings.
> He sees the same Truth everywhere,
> He sees the same God everywhere.

Meditation on the inner Self is not spiritualism. Particularly in the East, people are accustomed to invoking spirits and ghosts, and they think meditation is invoking the spirits, and that through meditation some miracles should take place. This is a common notion. But true meditation is not like this. We do not meditate to invoke spirits. We meditate to invoke the supreme Spirit, or God.

Baba Muktananda used to say that in the modern age people do not like to use the word "God." They speak of "Consciousness," "your full potential," "what you really are," or "the meditative energy." What can we do? This is the world we live in. In these days people don't seem able to take the Truth as it is. We have to change it in order to like it.

People meditate for different reasons: some people meditate to get over their illnesses, some to get over their limited thoughts. Students like to meditate so that they can pass their exams. But true meditation is becoming absorbed in the Truth at all times, in all places, with all people.

It is better not to place conditions on the results of meditation. God has placed everything within all of us. As we continue to meditate, we have different experiences at different times in our lives. Many people say, "When I first started meditating, I had so many visions and so many kinds of experiences. Now, five years later, there is nothing. I don't have any visions and I don't experience anything. It must be a dry spell."

Even though you think your experience is dry, still a great deal is happening. The power of meditation never stops. The fact that you do not experience anything at a particular moment does not mean that you should give up and do something else.

There was a farmer who wanted water, so he dug a well fifty feet deep. He didn't find any water, so he dug another fifty-foot well. Once again, no water. Three more times he dug to a depth of fifty feet. Still no water. Finally, he was exhausted, and he went to a wise sage. In the East people still go to a Master to ask about personal problems. The farmer told the sage what had happened.

The sage said, "Why did you dig five wells? Why didn't you stick to one and go deeper than fifty feet? You would have found water."

Keep going deeper and deeper. Do not limit the results of meditation.

A great saint, John of the Cross, said:

> That you may have pleasure in everything,
> Seek pleasure in nothing.
> That you may possess all things,
> Possess nothing.
> That you may be everything,
> Seek to be nothing.

This is the true way of life. If you want true pleasure, then do not go after pleasures. If you want to possess everything, do not go after anything. If you want to become something, first become nothing. That is true humility. Without true humility, it is very difficult to recognize the experiences that we have. Beautiful experiences are taking place within us, but we cannot see them if we lack humility. True humility is nothing but love, and love is nothing but respect.

A king asked his prime minister, "Tell me, what is the best thing in this world, and what is the worst thing?"

The prime minister said, "The tongue is both the best and the worst."

The king was curious. "How so?" he asked.

The prime minister replied, "With this tongue a human being can elevate the entire universe, and with this same tongue a human being can send this universe to hell."

Sometimes even though we feel good, we need to train the tongue to say good things. In Siddha Meditation, the way we train our tongue is by chanting the name of God over and over again. As chanting opens up the heart, it fills the entire being with great love.

The saint Kabir says:

What is the use of a life
Without the name of God, without chanting?
Let it be consumed by fire.
No matter how big a mountain is,
Without trees, it is desolate.
No matter how big a tree is,
Without leaves, it is barren.
Without a king, the subjects feel empty,
And a king without knowledge is incompetent.
Music without a melody is discordant,
And a melody without devotion is insipid.
A temple without a lamp is gloomy,
And a lamp without a flame is dark.
Kabir says, without the name of God,
What good is anyone's life?

Kabir's words are true. This planet is highly populated. When we want inner solace, where do we turn? We have created a lot of psychotherapists and a lot of counselors, but in the long run, how much can they do for us? They even get tired of taking our money. And if we do not go to them, we only suppress our feelings, which then come out in different physical conditions, and then we go to doctors instead. But if we have the flame of love burning within us, it consumes all our problems and negativities.

While chanting, rather than analyze the meaning, learn to lose yourself in the sound. Let it fill you completely. Make more room inside so that the sound can expand. In meditation too, just lose yourself. Do not worry about how well you are sitting or how bad your posture is. Just lose yourself in it. Baba used to say, "Do not be afraid of losing yourself. I will find you." The words of a Master are like a *koan*: they might sound simple, but they are full of meaning.

Lose yourself and become ecstatic. Become humble, and you will be filled with love. As you become filled with love, you will be able to respect one another, and thereby the word "respect" will gain great honor.

Bearing that in mind, with great love and great respect, I welcome you all with all my heart.
Sadgurunāth Mahārāj kī Jay!

The Secret of Action

Maui, Hawaii, December 28, 1985

WITH GREAT RESPECT AND LOVE, I welcome you all with all my heart. One of the great attractions for us here is to go to the Haleakala Crater and chant. Of course, the tourists and the rangers wonder what we are up to. In fact, when I arrived there this morning, a man who was leading his horse asked, "What are you singing?"

Someone answered, "We are chanting in Sanskrit."

He said, "My horse will go crazy if he hears that!"

If we don't like something, we blame it on someone else. We say, "It's my cat." "It's my horse." Our neighbors say, "Don't do that. My pet doesn't like it." "Don't do that. My child doesn't like it." "Don't do that. My spouse doesn't like it." It is always someone else.

We need to know what we are, what it is that exists within us, what it is that exists within others. Once we recognize what this is, then it does not matter where we live, where we go, or with whom we spend our lives. Then, whether we live among people or by ourselves, we will experience the same Truth, the same reality, and the same energy.

We cannot experience this energy until it has been awakened, and it is awakened by the grace of a Master. That is the way it happens. We can fool ourselves by saying, "If I do this technique, it will happen. If I read this book, it will happen. If I perform this austerity for forty years, it will happen." We do everything possible to avoid the Master. Isn't this so? Even if you have come here, you can still hide from grace, because you have developed a lot of techniques to avoid the inner awakening.

One of the best ways to become awakened is to receive the Word, the mantra, from the Master. Then the awakening of the energy happens instantaneously. A great being called Sundardas described his experience of how he received initiation:

> I went to my Master to receive initiation.
> What did he do?
> He gave me the fabulous Word.
> The moment he gave me the Word,
> It pierced my body.
> Just as the sun removes darkness,
> The Word removed my inner darkness,
>   my delusion.
> I am so grateful for this.
> With my entire being, with my speech,
>   with my mind,
> I offer my salutations to my Master.

When you receive something great from inside, gratitude wells up along with it. We lack gratitude in our lives even more than we lack the awakening of our inner energy. We receive so much from God, we receive so much from Nature, we receive so much from other people, yet we are ungrateful. Ingratitude causes most of the miseries in our lives, even more than ignorance of the inner Self. We take, take, take, but we never understand how much we have taken.

When we receive grace, it creates the grace of gratitude within us. This gratitude takes many forms: It takes the form of love and the form of compassion; it takes the form of a way of life. Gratitude gives life to living. Often we are dead while living, but gratitude brings us to life.

You think you perform action. Everyone performs actions; however, as Lord Krishna told Arjuna, you have to perform actions without desiring the fruits of your actions. As we act we often think, "What result is this going to bring about? How will I feel after I have finished it? How will someone else feel about my work?" This desire for the fruit of action hinders the true energy from performing your action. The Lord says to Arjuna:

> You have the right to work, but never to its fruits.
> Do not let the fruits of actions be your motive,
> Nor be attached to inaction.

When you work, just work. When you perform any action, just

perform it. People always asked Baba Muktananda, "If I work without having ambition, how will I achieve what I have set out to do?" But it is not ambition that accomplishes your work. When you perform work because it is your duty, then that duty accomplishes itself.

Ambition arises from ego. In Sanskrit the word for ambition means "the great destination" or "the great desire," and it is fine to have this kind of ambition. But usually our ambitions are not like this.

The Lord says, "Perform actions without any motive." Then the results are also great. When you perform actions without motive, you are not limited by your mind, by your ego, or by your intellect.

Once there was a fox who had lost one of his legs, so he could not go and get his own food. He had made friends with a tiger who brought him food every day. The tiger would hunt in the forest and eat half the food. Then he would give the rest to the fox.

A man who was walking through the forest saw what was happening. He was delighted. Every day he returned to watch the tiger bring food to the lame fox. He thought to himself, "This fox does not work. The tiger brings him food. I don't have to work either; I will also sit and someone will bring food. God will provide for me."

He sat down in the forest. Days passed by, and he began to lose a lot of weight. Finally he was near death. At the last minute a great voice from within suddenly boomed, "O man! Do not follow the fox. Follow the tiger!"

"Follow the tiger." The tiger was serving the fox without expectation of anything in return.

It is very important *how* we perform actions and what our goal is, yet there must be no motive and no desire. When we perform actions, let it not be out of desire, but from a sense of duty. If we must follow some example, let it be the greatest, the highest, the best. Many of us feel great when we see someone else having a hard time. It is not that we don't have any heart; it is just that when we see someone feeling sadder than we do, we feel better. However, in the *Bhagavad Gītā* the Lord says, "Follow in the footsteps of the great ones."

To be without desire does not mean becoming inactive. Action without a motive is inaction. Inaction with a motive is action. If you act without a motive, as the tiger did, you do not incur any consequences. But if inaction has a motive, then you suffer the consequences, as did the man who sat waiting and almost died as a result.

We have to understand how to live in this world. If we just look outside, then nothing will be gained from inside. If we only look inside, then nothing will be gained from the outside. We have to bring about a balance between action and inaction. For this, we have to know what we are, what is inside us, and what is inside others.

The Lord says to Arjuna:

> O Arjuna, perform action, being steadfast in yoga,
> Abandoning attachment, and balanced
>   in success and failure.
> Evenness of mind is called yoga.

"Evenness of mind is called yoga." Many of you must have heard this often: Evenness, a balanced state of mind, is the true union with God and with life. And so you put on a mask of being peaceful and tranquil — until someone steps on your toes. Then it is as though a spring were being released, and everything that has been suppressed inside in the name of peace and tranquility comes out.

The Lord says, "Perform action, being steadfast in yoga." For this attitude and this attainment, the inner and the outer have to be balanced. Evenness of mind means that you are happy during a happy moment and you are also happy during an unhappy moment. It is easy to be happy when everything is great, and it is easy to be unhappy when everything is going wrong. Evenness of mind comes to our aid in times of unhappiness and misery.

Many people, particularly reporters, used to ask Baba, "What have you done for the suffering of humanity?" It is amazing. We always ask this question of someone who teaches meditation or is a spiritual teacher, but we have never looked to see what we ourselves have done for the suffering of humanity. We always want to know what everyone else has done.

Baba was always fascinated by this question. In his life, he did what he could, and the best thing he did was never to boast about it. However, we disciples can boast about the Master. Baba helped the poor people in the way that he could help them, and he also helped the rich people in the way that he could help them. He helped humanity in general in the way that he could.

To the poor he gave clothes, milk, food, and houses. The mobile hospital that he created for them still travels to the villages every day, and both Westerners and Indians work on it. Whenever people needed inner healing, he gave that. To those who came to him as seekers of knowledge, he gave knowledge and wisdom. To those who came seeking love, he gave love. To those who came just seeking his company, he gave that.

Helping the suffering of humanity is done in many ways. In order to help, you must have been helped yourself. Baba always said, "If you don't have love, how can you give love to others?" It would be like Nasrudin's bank.

Sheik Nasrudin is a great character. Those of you who are new to Siddha Meditation should know that Sheik Nasrudin is a character used to depict everyone's life — at his own expense. If I mention someone's name and say he has this fault or that fault, everyone else feels, "Oh, that person must be feeling so bad!" But if I substitute Sheik Nasrudin's name, no one has to feel bad. Although we say it is Nasrudin, inside we know it applies to us also. But in this way nobody else will find out.

Once Sheik Nasrudin opened a bank, and he put up a big sign which read: Free Loans! No Interest! Everyone Welcome!

Free loans! Who in this world does not want a free loan? Five hundred people were standing in line before the bank had even opened.

Nasrudin came out of the bank. He climbed up on a bench and said, "My brothers and sisters! I welcome you all to my bank. Yes! Free loans, no interest. As soon as there is money in the bank, I will let you know."

Baba said most of us are like this. "As soon as I have it, I will give it to you." If you don't have it, what can you give? How can you help the suffering of humanity if you yourself have not been helped inside? Being helped does not just mean being fed or clothed or housed; it means being helped deep within. When all the suppressed *samskāras*, the impressions of many, many lifetimes, have been uprooted from within us, only *then* can we really help.

Whenever a reporter asked what Baba had done for the suffering of humanity, Baba would laugh and laugh. The reporter would say, "Don't avoid the question!" And Baba would laugh again. This was his greatness — no matter what, he could laugh. He did not just laugh it off; he really laughed, with the greatest joy, the highest bliss.

Then Baba would say, "I am so glad you asked this question. I am going to think about this."

The reporter would feel great that he had awakened this Master to the reality of humanity. By giving that answer, Baba removed the suffering of that reporter. "Evenness of mind is called yoga." When you have evenness of mind, you understand and experience the depth within. Your very being removes suffering within yourself and also outside you.

> Endowed with evenness of mind,
> One casts off in this life
> Both good and evil deeds.
> Therefore, devote yourself to yoga.
> Yoga is skill in action.

When the mind has become even and can accept both good and evil, that mind is fit to perform action. Yoga is skill in action. When you perform actions, those actions contain a lot of consequences. To face them, we need evenness of mind.

A seeker went to see Lord Buddha and asked for initiation. Buddha said, "You are not ready for it yet."

The seeker asked, "Why?"

We go to the Master to find out what we are, but when the Master says something we ask why!

Lord Buddha replied, "You are not ready. That is why."

"But why am I not ready?"

"Because you are still affected by everything."

"How can I get over being affected by everything?"

"Come tomorrow."

The seeker returned the next day, and Lord Buddha said to him, "Go to the graveyard and praise the dead. Use the most flattering terms you can think of. Praise them to the utmost."

The seeker said, "All right." He went to the graveyard and started praising every ancestor, every relative. "How wonderful you were! How beautiful! How great! How incredible! How superb!" When he returned, Lord Buddha said, "Now go and yell at them. Scream at the top of your lungs. Revile them for everything bad that they have done."

The seeker thought, "Well, I asked for it." He went back to the graveyard. He started yelling and shouting at them. He used every foul term he could think of.

Again when he went back, Lord Buddha asked him, "What did they say to you when you praised them?"

The seeker said, "Nothing."

"What did they say to you when you yelled at them?"

"Nothing."

Lord Buddha said, "When you become nothing, you will be fit for initiation. Go. Become nothing." With that, the seeker was enlightened. He didn't have to do a lot to become nothing. When grace flows from the Master, it just happens.

Last night after my talk a man said to me, "Gurumayi, I am ready."

I said, "Very good."

He said, "Did you hear me? I am ready."

You are so ready, yet you have a doubt whether the person that you are talking to heard you or not. I just nodded my head, and he walked away. He came back ten minutes later.

I said, "You have come back."

He said, "Yes. I just want you to know I am ready."

I said, "Very good."

He said, "Give it to me."

I said, "Very good."

I like yearning and readiness, but you cannot *demand* the awakening that happens within. It is so subtle, yet so powerful. It happens through grace.

We sit for meditation for hours on end, but meditation does not happen for hours on end. There is a fraction of a moment, a split second, very brief, very subtle, when everything happens. But by sitting for hours, day after day, night after night, we prepare our body to experience action in inaction and inaction in action. Meditation is a great method of preparation, because even though you are not doing anything, a lot is happening. And although you are doing a lot, nothing is happening. It is action in inaction, and inaction in action. Meditation is a wonderful technique. There comes a point where we lose our awareness; and in that losing, there is absolute awareness. It is so fine and so subtle. It is the source of inspiration, of life, of everything that we do, and it is the source of the awakening.

People do hatha yoga to awaken the inner energy, even though hatha yoga itself originally came about from the awakening of that energy. In Ganeshpuri when people received Shaktipat from Baba, they would have dramatic physical experiences. In fact, if I talked about them right now, you might panic. However, I will talk about them anyway. Perhaps when you panic you will experience something!

Some people, when they received Shaktipat, would suddenly stand on their heads, not just for a few seconds but for many hours. Visitors would be terrified. "What is going on in this place?"

Can you imagine? You have never heard about yoga or spirituality or the inner Self, and all of a sudden you see someone standing on his head! But that posture undoubtedly has great benefits. We don't know what illness, mental or physical, we carry in our system. But the energy knows. When it is awakened, it goes right to where the work is needed; it does not waste any time. When these illnesses are worked on and removed, the final experience takes place: We know the bliss of perceiving the Supreme constantly, inside and outside, the bliss of finding the true Beloved. Then there is neither hatred nor attraction, just the purest form of love. Therefore, Kabir said:

Remove the veil.
You will find your Beloved within.
In every heart the Lord dwells.
Therefore, speak no bitter words.
The One who listens within you
Also listens within everyone else.

This veil is the ego. This veil is impurity, sickness, and suffering. As we remove the veil, we find our true Beloved; we find the Truth inside.

Lord Krishna says:

O Arjuna, that person excels
Who controls the senses by the mind,
And who engages in action with the organs of action,
Without attachment.

When this inner awakening takes place, attachment is removed. Attachment and suffering go hand in hand. When we are separated from the action we perform, the result is always as it should be. It is not tainted by what we *think* it should be.

Go deep within and find your Beloved. When the awakening takes place, do not block it with your idea of a religion, your idea of a path, your idea of meditation.

There was a great being who was a Moslem. In the Islamic religion, they do not believe in the form of God, only in the formless. This great being was having the final realization in a vision of the Blue Pearl, which appeared before him as a very tiny bright light.

The Blue Pearl began to expand and expand, and it took on a form made up of thousands and millions of scintillating dots. It was incredibly

14

beautiful. Being a Moslem, he could not believe that he was seeing a form. So he panicked: he broke into a sweat, screamed, and ran out of the room.

He had heard about Baba and knew that Baba believed in the form of God. So he sent his secretary to Baba to ask if he was being possessed.

Baba was delighted to hear the man's experience, but he said, "He was going to get realized! How could he have stopped it?"

The secretary replied, "But Swamiji, don't you understand? In our religion we do not believe in the form of God."

Baba said, "How could a person waste such a realization in the name of religion? How could he let religion get in the way? How does he know what the founder of the religion experienced, anyway? He might not have written his experiences down. So you just throw it away? Tell him not to stop his experience. He should meditate again, and he will have the realization."

The secretary went back and told the great being what Baba had said, but he replied, "Tcht! If people found out that I had become realized through a form of God, I would be thrown out of my religion. It is better not to have any experience and just continue to do what I have been doing."

Don't let a religion, the idea of religion, or the idea of a path stop you. Baba often said, "So many great beings did not write down every experience, and even if they did, they used enigmatic words or aphorisms. And it is difficult to understand these aphorisms unless you have had that experience."

The Koran says that God, Allah, is everywhere. How could He be everywhere and not in a form? To know that God exists in water and also in the process of water evaporating, you need to have that experience. He exists in both. This is why you should perform your duty and not worry about the consequences. Then you gain inaction in action, and action in inaction.

> O Arjuna, he who through the likeness
> of the Self
> Sees equality everywhere,
> whether in pleasure or in pain,
> Is regarded as the highest yogi.

Experiencing the same in pleasure as in pain, experiencing joy from pain, does not mean masochism. It is the joy called "unmixed happiness," joy which is not tainted or stained. This joy exists independently of pleasure and pain; it exists for its own sake.

> There is nothing whatsoever higher
>   than I am, O Arjuna!
> All this is strung on Me like clusters
>   of gems on a string.

In every holy book, you come across this teaching. "I am that I am." "I am the Way." "There is nothing whatsoever higher than 'I am,' O Arjuna."

The yogis and seers who went deep within said that "I am" is the awareness "I am That," *So'ham,* "I am the Truth," "I am Reality." This "I" is not the small self, the body, the mind, or the intellect. It is the supreme "I," the "I" which is beyond the limitations of the ego, the mind, and the senses. Through meditation we become absorbed in this "I," the great "I," which Shaivism calls *Pūrno'ham vimarsha,* the "perfect 'I'-consciousness."

Lord Krishna continues:

> I am the wetness in water,
>   the light in the moon and the sun,
> I am the syllable *Om* in all the scriptures,
>   sound in ether, and virility in men.
> I am the sweet fragrance in the earth,
>   the brilliance in fire,
> The life in all beings,
>   and austerity in ascetics.
> O Arjuna, know Me as the eternal seed of all beings,
>   the intelligence of the intellect,
> And the splendor of splendid objects.
> I am the One in everything and in everyone.

To recognize this "I am," we have to dive deep within through meditation. As we meditate and become meditation, we become the Way. As we chant and become chanting, we become the Way. As we perform our duties and become the duty, we become the Way. Then this separation between the Lord and the devotee vanishes. The Master and the disciple and all people become one. As all rivers merge into the ocean, we all merge into the ocean of the Truth.

Keep practicing until you merge with the Truth, and after you merge you will continue your practices just for the joy of it. Then your joy will be everyone else's joy. It will help to remove the suffering of humanity — not just the suffering that you think of as suffering, but the more profound suffering of which you are not even aware. When that happens, this earth itself becomes paradise.

When I was in Japan, someone told me, "It is my understanding that this earth is heaven and this earth is hell. What do they think in Siddha Yoga?"

I said, "Very good. We think that too. But we also do something about it. We meditate and we chant, so that this earth can be paradise all the time, and not just sometimes."

We will chant the mantra *Om Namah Shivāya*. Those who have had the experience of becoming one with nature, of listening to the birds sing and to the sound of running water, and of inhaling the fragrance of the earth, must have experienced this sound, *Om, Om*. In the old shrines they play big cymbals, and they make the same sound, *Om, Om*. When you merge inside, you will feel these cymbals playing. Many of you think it is a disease and go to a doctor. It is good to get your hearing checked, but the sound also happens when you start experiencing what is inside you and what is inside the universe.

A father and mother came to a program in Manhattan. Their daughter has been meditating for six or seven years. When the chant began, they were horrified. They ran out of the hall and stood in the lobby. As they waited in the lobby, they began to like the chant, so very slowly they crept back in again.

They went home and wrote me a letter in which they said, "We were so afraid when we first heard the sound of the chanting." They were quite old, seventy or seventy-five, and they said their eardrums had become weak. "But," they told me, "as soon as the sound went into our bodies, we felt very calm. We felt a soothing energy. Our anxiety began to settle down, and we felt wonderful."

If you do not think the sound of the chanting is quite right when you first hear it, just have a little patience. Then the cymbals will ring inside, and you will hear the sound "I am" — just "I am," *Pūrno'ham*. Become absorbed in the sweetness of that awareness. Let the mind play its tricks, let it perform its actions while you, as the Truth, become one with the Truth. Let your whole being merge into it.

As we sing *Om Namah Shivāya*, let the sound reverberate throughout your being. Let every cell hear the sound of the words. Then after we stop chanting aloud, we will sit quietly. You do not need to do anything. This is the beauty of Baba's Siddha Meditation: it is the power of grace. Just because we think we must do something, Baba said repeat the mantra mentally, sit up straight, and cross your legs. But if you can accept the fact that grace is natural, then the awakening takes place spontaneously.

Don't be like the man who stopped the experience. Let it happen. We are all human beings.

With great respect and with great love, I welcome you all with all my heart.

Sadgurunāth Mahārāj kī Jay!

Patience: A New Year's Resolution

Honolulu, January 1, 1986

WITH GREAT RESPECT AND LOVE, I welcome you all with all my heart. There is a story about an Ayurvedic physician who wanted to test all his students, so he took the form of a bird and perched on the branch of a tree beside a river in which they were bathing. He began to caw, *"Kora ruk, kora ruk,"* which means, "Who is healthy? Who is healthy?"

One of the students said, "One who crushes pearls and makes a paste of the powder, and takes a little drop of that every morning remains healthy."

Another said, "One who eats a bit of pig's liver every afternoon stays very healthy."

Each student gave a different answer, but the teacher was not satisfied. After one hundred students had given different answers, there was one who said, *"Hitabhuk, mitabhuk, ritabhuk."* *Hitabhuk* means that he who eats what is beneficial for him remains very healthy. *Mitabhuk* means that he who eats moderately, only what the body needs, remains healthy. *Ritabhuk* means that he who eats according to the season remains healthy. In India there are three seasons: summer, winter, and monsoon. In summer, one eats a particular type of food; in winter, another; and in monsoon, yet another.

Hearing this answer, the doctor was satisfied. He said, "It is not medicine that is going to cure you. It is how you eat, how you behave, and how you think that will really affect your body, your mind, your soul, and your entire life."

Some people celebrate New Year's Eve by getting drunk; they go from one bar to another. Then on New Year's Day they are ill in bed, and they wonder, "How am I going to survive another year?"

True health is hitabhuk, mitabhuk, and ritabhuk, and this principle applies to our spiritual life as well. Many of us think meditation is so good for us that we meditate for six or eight hours a day. But without moderation, meditation, instead of being beneficial, becomes the reverse.

When Baba was at the DeVille in South Fallsburg, New York, two students of meditation came to visit him. They were frail and pallid. They asked Baba, "If meditation is so great, then why do we look like this? We meditate eight hours a day. We do *prānāyāma*" — breath control. "We do all the *āsanas*" — the postures — "and we sit very quietly for so many hours."

Baba looked at them and asked, "When do you eat?"

They were astounded. "But Baba," they said, "you are a meditation teacher. Why do you talk about eating?"

Baba asked, "When do you eat?"

They said, "Once a day, at five in the evening."

Baba said, "That is not how the body is made. When you were inside your mother's womb, she ate a great deal. Don't you remember?"

We are trying to attain the highest, yet we forget the simplest teaching. On the spiritual path, the teacher brings us back to what is simple, to what we really are. The body is made up of five elements: earth, water, fire, wind, and ether. To keep these five elements in their proper balance you must have food. Because the body is made up of the earth element, food is necessary. If we call ourselves meditators or spiritual people, it is very important that we remember hitabhuk, mitabhuk, and ritabhuk.

There are different phases in meditation. One day you feel great; another day, dry. When you feel great, you think you are great. But when your meditation is dry, you think *you* are dry and you give up meditation. You say, "Meditation is supposed to fill me with juice, but I feel so dry." Then you go looking for vodka or beer to juice yourself up.

In the *Aparokshānubhūti*, a great scripture which talks about discipline and philosophy, it is said:

> Those people who are merely clever at discussing God,
> But who have no direct realization,
> And who are very much attached to worldly pleasures,
> Take birth and die again and again as a result of ignorance.

If you are only clever at theorizing about God, the Truth, or the Self, you do not attain any of them. You need the practical aspect of *sādhanā*, the direct realization of God. Without this direct realization, there is no attainment. We read and read, we listen and listen, yet we do not feel anything because we have neglected the practical aspect. Without direct realization, theory cannot really do much to help us.

Therefore, in the *Aparokshānubhūti* Shankaracharya says:

A person who is qualified
And who desires his own good,
Should engage in constant self-inquiry
In order to attain knowledge.

For a lot of people, self-inquiry is scary. They feel, "If I start looking into myself, I will come across so many things that I do not need to know. Ignorance is bliss."

When I was coming here this evening, someone said to me, "Another Happy New Year to celebrate the year of ignorance."

I asked, "Why do you say that?"

The person said, "Well, this is how everyone lives — in the year of ignorance."

We keep celebrating our ignorance. When you practice self-inquiry, you realize that even though you are on the spiritual path, you are celebrating another year of ignorance. I am certain that tonight a lot of people will say, "Gurumayi, I have been meditating for the last thirteen years, but nothing has happened. I have been thinking about God for so long, but I haven't received a boon."

When you start self-inquiry you are flooded with memories and thoughts. At the beginning of the year, the newspapers and magazines give a summary of what happened in the previous year. They highlight all the accidents, deaths, hijackings, airplane crashes, murders, and robberies. We think, "Another year of all that?" Then we become sad.

In the same way, self-inquiry can cause sadness. Nevertheless, the scriptures say if you keep probing deeper, you go beyond superficial calamities and discover the true gem that is within: God, the Truth, the Self.

Once King Janaka was taking his afternoon nap, and he began to dream that another king invaded his country. He lost the battle, but the enemy king let him go and did not put him in prison. While wandering, Janaka became so hungry that he went into a field and began to eat the corn. The farmer saw a man stealing his crops, so he picked up a stick and began to beat him.

When Janaka woke up, he was in the palace in his bed, and all his servants were fanning him. He closed his eyes and he was back in the field — the farmer was thrashing him. He woke up and he was back in the palace in his bed. He sat up, absolutely confused: "Which is real, my dream or my waking state?" Both were so vivid and so clear.

He began to practice self-inquiry, but he could not arrive at an answer. So the next day he went to the court and called for all the sages and seers. When they arrived he put this question to them: "Tell me: Which is real — my dream or my waking state?"

Then he explained to them what had happened. All the sages and seers gave him different answers, but he was not satisfied. So he put them in jail.

A few years passed. Then a little sage living in the kingdom asked his mother, "Where is my father? Why have I never seen him?"

The mother said, "Your father is in jail."

The boy asked, "Why?"

She said, "The king asked a question and he could not answer it."

"What kind of question?" the little boy asked. When his mother told him, he replied, "I will answer that question," and he went to the court.

This young sage's body was twisted in eight places, and so he was called *Ashtavakra*. As he entered the court, all the courtiers began to laugh at him because of the strange way he walked.

Then the king, too, started laughing, but the boy was not affected by their laughter. Since Ashtavakra was a sage, the king put him beside him on his throne.

The king asked, "Are you ready for my question, O young sage?"

"Not yet," Ashtavakra said. "First I need to ask *you* a question. Then I will answer your question."

"That is all right," the king said.

The young sage asked, "O Your Majesty, I can understand why everyone else was laughing, but can you tell me why *you* were laughing when I walked in?"

The king was stunned; however, he had to answer the question. "O sage," he said, "what can I say? I saw your crooked body. I had never seen anything like it before in my life, so I laughed."

The young sage said, "O Your Majesty, if your eyes can see only what is external, how can you understand that Truth which is more hidden than the hidden, subtler than the subtlest, finer than the finest? You are blind, O King. You are looking only at the body, not at what is inside the body. Even if I were to answer your question, if all you could see was my body, how would you understand what I was saying?"

At that point the king was enlightened. Until then his eyes had perceived only what was external, not what was inside. He sat in great humility. When he was ripe and ready to listen to the Truth, Ashtavakra said, "O Your Majesty, as long as you are ignorant and bound, both states — what you see in your dream state and what you see in your waking state — are real. However, when you become enlightened, neither of these states is real. Only the highest state is the true reality. If you rise above both these states of bondage — being beaten by the farmer and lying in the royal bed — then you will know that you are a different being: You are the Self; you are the Truth."

When you practice self-inquiry, it takes you higher and it takes you deeper. When you do not do any self-inquiry, you do not become ripe to hear the Truth or to attain the Truth. You do not become eligible for that experience.

Shankaracharya continues:

> The Self is pure Consciousness and holy,
> Whereas the body is of flesh and impure.
> Yet people confuse these two
> And consider them as one.
> What else but this can be called ignorance?

We confuse the Self with the body. Meditation on the Self is not meditation on the body.

Someone asked me the other day, "How can I meditate on the Truth when I do not know what the Truth is?"

We might not know what the Truth is in its abstract sense, yet there is Truth happening in our everyday life. Kahlil Gibran says: "I discovered the secret of the sea in meditation on the dewdrop." If we can focus on something very small, then that focus will take us to the highest and greatest. But we must see beyond the physical realm. For this we must meditate, for this we need inner experience.

Meditation on the Self is not meditation on the body. It is not meditation on the tip of the nose or on the earlobes or on the fingernails. Meditation on the Self is beyond what is transitory, yet you can attain it through the transitory elements. You can meditate on a dewdrop, which is transitory, and it will reveal the secrets of the ocean. You can meditate on a spark, and it will reveal the secrets of fire. You can meditate on your breath; it will reveal the secrets of the wind. You can meditate on ether; it will reveal the secrets of pure Consciousness.

Meditation on the transitory elements can take you to the highest, but if you get stuck in them, that is a problem.

Just as when clouds move,
The moon appears to be in motion,
Similarly, because of ignorance
A person sees the Self as the body.

When the clouds move, we think the moon is moving. In Vedanta there are a lot of other descriptions of this kind of folly; they also say it is like seeing a snake in a rope.

Once there was a man who was walking at night. When he saw a crooked object lying in the middle of the road, he began to scream and shout, "A snake! A snake! Help! Help!"

Some people came running with a flashlight. They said, "This is not a snake; it is just a rope."

"Oh!" he said. "I thought it was a snake."

Because he thought it was a snake, he experienced fear. But once he realized it was just a rope, everything was fine.

Then another man came walking down the road shouting, "Stop, thief! Stop, thief!"

Everyone came running with flashlights and asked, "Where is the thief?"

"Here!"

They shone the light on the object. It was just a tree trunk.

As long as the man thought it was a thief, he, too, experienced fear. Once he realized it was a tree trunk, everything was fine.

We are afraid because we think of this world as something other than what it is, we think of people as something other than what they are. We think of ourselves as something other than what we are. Fear causes doubts and negativities and eventually brings about our downfall. The only way you can fall is by being fraught with fear, because when you doubt yourself, you also doubt your friends, and the world in which you are living seems threatening. You are afraid to meditate on your own Self, to practice self-inquiry, because you are scared that you will discover what is inside. However, Kahlil Gibran says: "When I planted my pain in the field of patience, it bore the fruit of happiness."

Hitabhuk, mitabhuk, ritabhuk. Do what is beneficial, do it in moderation, and do it at the right time, in the right place. At the beginning of another year, learn to have patience. If you have patience, you will know how to eat, how to think, how to dress, how to live. You will speak to those people to whom it is necessary to speak, and hear only what it is necessary to hear. You will keep within yourself only what it is necessary to keep. To everything else, you will say good-bye.

So for another year, whether it is a happy or sad year in your mind, have patience. Through patience, you attain everything. If you have patience you can meditate or work, be alone or make friends. If you have patience, you can live a true life.

Without patience, calamities arise. When the ocean has no patience, flood after flood occurs. When the wind has no patience, storm after storm rages. In the same way, if we have no patience, we squander our energy in all directions. When we have patience we have contentment, and through contentment we become even more patient.

Once you have patience you can meditate on your own Self; you can worship your own Self, kneel to your own Self, understand your own Self, respect your own Self. And you have the time to experience that God dwells within you as you.

Kahlil Gibran says: "My enemy said to me, 'Love your enemy.' And I obeyed him and loved myself." This is very profound. In the *Bhagavad Gītā* the Lord says, "You are your own friend; you are your own enemy." When there is no fear, you are your own friend. When there is fear, you are your own enemy.

The *Aparokshānubhūti* says:

> People perform all their actions in and through God,
> But because of ignorance, they are not aware of it,
> Just as through ignorance people do not know
> That pottery is nothing but earth.

All our actions are performed in the Truth, by the Truth, and for the Truth. This is the wisdom of the enlightened beings. When we are bound, we do not have this knowledge, nor do we have this experience.

Meditate on the Self, which is eternal. No matter how many doubts you may have, the Self does not have any doubts. No matter how many negativities you may have, the Self has no negativities. No matter how tired your body may be, the Self is never tired. The Self is everywhere and in everything. If you do not know what the Truth is, then meditate on a flower, meditate on a particle of dust, meditate on a spark, meditate on a leaf, meditate on one of the designs in the carpet. Meditate on anything, and it will take you through.

Faith does bear fruit. Patience does bear fruit. And do not think of meditation as being only one technique or another. Keep meditation unconditional, and it will mold your life.

For the coming year make the resolution, "I will have patience." Patience, absolute patience. Have no doubt, patience will bring all the treasures hidden in the rainbow. It will.

Kabir said:

> O my dear one, where are you looking for Me?
> I am with you.
> Don't think I live just in your bones or flesh.
> Don't think I live just in your hair.
> I am with you constantly.
> Where are you looking for Me?
> Don't look for Me in a temple,
> Don't look for Me in a mosque,
> Don't look for Me in a holy place,
> Don't look for Me in a holy river.
> I don't live in these places.
> I live in your trust,
> I live in your faith.

This is true. We see time and time again where God dwells, where the Truth dwells, where the Self dwells: it is in our love, our faith, and our trust. When we lack these qualities, we have no experience of God. It is not that God ceases to exist, but He does not exist for *us*.

Kabir says:

> Find Me in your trust;
> Find Me in your faith.
> I don't live in ceremonies;
> I don't live in renunciation.
> Nor do I live in *sannyāsa*.
> If you look for Me, you will find Me.
> I live in your search.

Many people think that if they give up their houses and their families and become renunciates, they will find God. Then they look at the renunciates to see if they have found the Truth, and when they see that they haven't, they say sarcastically, "This is just a mirage, a fantasy. There is nothing in it." Then they go about their daily lives leaving out God, leaving out the Truth, leaving out spirituality.

Kabir says: Do not look for Me in renunciation; do not look for Me in sannyasa, in monkhood. I exist in your search itself. So whoever seeks the Truth does find it.

Many people used to say to Baba, "Baba, I meditate but nothing happens."

Baba was always amused by this. He said, "You tell me you are meditating and nothing is happening. How is that possible? If you are meditating, it's happening!"

Many people say, "I am searching but I haven't found anything." What they are looking for is in their search, but they expect to find it somewhere else. Isn't it true that we never see what is closest to us? It happens every day. "I can't find my glasses!" we say, while our glasses are in our pocket. "Have you seen where I put my glasses? The last place I left them was on my table." Do we ever look for them in our hands? No. The object of the search is within the seeker. In his song Kabir says: When you look, you will find the Lord in a second, because He is in your very search.

Kabir compares the body to a city. He says:

Do not think My abode is outside the city.
I am in your breath;
I am with you.
Kabir says, O my dear ones, listen to me!
What you are searching for is with you constantly.

Meditate on your own Self. Worship your own Self. Kneel to your own Self. Respect your own Self. Understand your own Self. God dwells within you as you.

Someone came up to Baba and asked, "Are you God?"

Baba said, " Just as you are God, I am too."

When you have the experience, you realize that as much as anyone else is God, you are God, too. It is not just the outer body that is God, it is the inner attainment of each person. The inner attainment is nothing but the Truth. For this reason, when you read the words of the enlightened ones, you find that no matter what country or period of time they lived in, they were all similar, and the Truth they experienced was the same.

The object of the search exists in the search itself. The one who is seeking is himself the object of his search. So meditate on your own Self.

For another year — a happy, happy New Year — we will have patience. Every practice in Siddha Yoga — the *Guru Gītā*, waiting for your meals and your shoes, the evening chant, the evening program — develops patience. Many people do not know what these practices can do for them. What they can do is cultivate patience in each seeker, who is the object of his or her own search.

With great respect and with great love, once again I welcome you all with all my heart.

Sadgurunāth Mahārāj kī Jay!

In the Cave of the Heart

Oakland, California, February 4, 1986

WITH GREAT RESPECT AND LOVE, I welcome you all with all my heart. Talking about the basic questions of life, Bholenath sings:

> If you do not understand the simple matters of life,
> Then you live in great ignorance.
> Have you ever asked yourself,
> "Where have I come from?
> Where must I go?
> What am I supposed to do here?
> What am I supposed to know?"
> Have you ever tried to understand what love is all about?
> Have you ever known what compassion is?
> If you have not contemplated and experienced these things,
> Then you are living in great ignorance.

We consider ourselves wonderful philosophers because we so often ask: "Who am I? Where have I come from?" But as soon as some distraction arises, we forget about finding the answer.

If you ask a child, "Where do you come from?" the child's answer is, "From my parents."

If you ask, "Where do your parents come from?" then he starts to wonder.

Sometimes when people come to see me, I ask them, "Where do you come from?"

They say, "The West Coast."

If I say, "Where on the West Coast?"

They answer, "California."

"That is a big state. Where do you come from in California?"

They tell me, "Los Angeles."

"Ahh, Los Angeles." Once again, Los Angeles is a big city. So the questions can be endless.

However, according to the philosophers, the answer to the question "Where are you from?" is not a person or a time or a place.

Many people believe in past lives. They go to a psychic and ask, "Where was I in my last incarnation?" The psychic closes his or her eyes for a few minutes, feels the energy, sees the aura, and says, "You were born in Egypt!" Then a great revelation comes up inside you: "Ahh. No wonder I behave the way I do! I don't belong here — I belong somewhere else!"

We get quite tied up in this question of "Where am I from?" For this reason, Bholenath says you must have the knowledge, the understanding, that comes from turning within. We look for answers outside: from other people, other things, other places. And for a while those answers give us a good feeling. However, because we do not make our inner foundation strong, we gain no lasting satisfaction; we do not become established in the inner experience.

"Where do I come from?" In the beginning, we are just a drop. Before that drop, we were nothing. The scriptures say that we come from that nothingness. We were no body; we were no thing. To have the experience of the Truth, we have to go back to that nothingness.

There was a salt doll who wanted to know herself. She walked for hundreds of miles until finally she came to the ocean. When she saw the ocean, she was fascinated. She had never seen such a thing. She went closer to it and asked, "What are you?"

The ocean said, "Enter me and you will find out."

She wanted the answer, so she walked in. As she walked further and further into the water, she began to dissolve. When only a tiny bit of her remained, she said, "Now I know what I am."

The only way to experience the Truth, or Reality, is to become nothing. Having experienced nothingness, when you become a human being once again, you are able to live the real life. Otherwise, you experience only delusion, or *māyā*.

Where have I come from
And what have I brought with me?

What have we brought with us? We talk a lot, and we come up

with a lot of ideas: "I'm this; I'm that." "I want to do this or that." "I want to give this person this; I want to give that person that." "I want to make this person happy, and I am going to ruin that person's life." We keep saying all these things, but what did we bring with us when we came?

> Having come here,
> What are we going to take with us?

These are major questions: What did we bring with us when we were born? And what shall we take with us when we die?

While Baba was doing his *sādhanā*, he did the practices and performed austerities, he fasted and lived in rags, and he went from place to place searching for the Truth. He did everything from scratch. Having attained the Truth, he then received the command from his Guru to give what he had attained to others.

From that point on, so much began to happen. But you can't just sit by the roadside and give the teachings as they did in the past. If you are in the city, you have to give shelter. And when you give shelter, then others want to help with that. As time goes on, all that some people can see is other human beings and a huge building. This is maya. We get totally lost in it and the Truth is hidden in our delusion.

We have to drop the veil of delusion. When we came we brought nothing with us. And whatever we find here is for this world only. However, if we realize the Truth and merge into it, we take that with us, and we are reborn with that knowledge. This is why some people are born realized or enlightened.

What do we bring, and what do we take with us? Only knowledge. And if this knowledge is not purified, then when we are reborn we bring delusion with us. Memory is not erased when we take birth or die. It remains. The body lives through the power of memory, so memory has to be purified through the power of knowledge.

The *Yoga Vāsishtha* says:

> There is no fear of destruction
> In a battle painted on a canvas.
> Similarly, when the knower of the Truth
> Is established in inner equanimity,
> Activity does not affect him.

"There is no fear of destruction in a battle painted on a canvas."

This is the fruit of the experience of the Truth. If our life falls apart, we panic because we take that as reality. If someone pays us a compliment, we take that as reality and we feel great. If we have a lover, we feel complete. If we lose our lover, we feel incomplete. Our life goes up and down. Our sense of our perfection depends on what others say, instead of being an independent experience of our own perfection, our own completeness.

The sage says that when you have the experience of the Truth, you see everything as an illusion. Once you understand that everything is an illusion, then paradoxically you can see everything as the Truth. Then, whether we are complimented or insulted, we are not shaken up; there is steadiness.

This steadiness comes about through practice and dispassion. Practice is essential. In Hawaii, we saw people jogging every day. Regardless of whether they were thin or fat, the same people jogged day after day, while others went swimming. One person got stung by a jellyfish, but the next day she was swimming again. They did the practice, and they got the joy out of it. But we need practices which will take us deeper than our muscles and bones, because muscles and bones won't last long, no matter how sturdy they are now. We need the deeper knowledge which arises through the practice of meditation.

The sages developed many techniques to bring about the stillness of the mind. Some focused their eyes on the rising or setting sun, others on the tips of their noses or on different parts of their body, and still others visualized a tiny dot on which they focused their attention.

Different sages and seers performed different techniques. However, before practicing these techniques, they received grace. Without grace, all techniques are dry. This is why a lot of people do not want to do the practices. The practices have become mechanical; they do not have *rasa* or joy. What brings joy to the practices is grace.

Baba gave us a very simple technique. He said, ''Just close your eyes, and you will have the experience of God.'' This is the simple truth. Just by closing your eyes, you can find the Truth.

For those who could not do that, he said, ''Chant the mantra.'' As you chant more and more, you awaken every cell in the body, and then the inner music is revealed.

A Sufi saint said that he used to laugh at people who moved their bodies continually. ''However,'' he said, ''I stopped laughing at them when I heard the inner music, because it began to happen to me.'' You can laugh at others who become engrossed in the inner music only if you yourself have not heard it.

In Ganeshpuri there was an older man who used to cook for Baba. After he finished cooking, he would sit on one of the steps, his head going around and around very gently, almost as if the wind were making it move. A lot of visitors couldn't understand this, so they would laugh and make fun of him. He had his eyes closed and was just humming to himself, totally engrossed, happy and joyful. Just by looking at him, you could feel your heart throb.

One day someone asked Baba, "Swamiji, why does that man act so strangely?"

Baba said, "Because he's *got it.*"

Where have we come from? What did we bring with us? What will we take with us when we go? We must understand this. We are very curious to know about everyone else, but never about ourselves. We want what others have externally, but we never think about wanting what others have deep inside. Look for what is deep inside. That is what we brought with us, that is what we will take with us, and that is what we give to one another.

Once we have the knowledge of the Truth, then there is no fear of destruction in a battlefield painted on a canvas.

In the *Paramārthasāra* it is said:

> As soon as a person acquires true knowledge,
> His actions no longer bear fruit.
> How could he then be reborn?
> Not being associated any longer
> With the bondage of birth,
> He reveals himself by the rays of the Self.
> He is the sun which is Shiva, the Lord.

Once you understand the Truth, your actions do not bear fruit. This is a frightening idea for those who believe in actions and reactions. "How can it be," they wonder, "that if I pray, I am not going to get the fruit of my prayer? If I do something good, won't I get the rewards of what I do?" But once actions are burnt up in the fire of knowledge, they can no longer bear fruit. When this happens to a person, the sages say, wherever he walks, every stone becomes a wish-fulfilling stone; every tree becomes a wish-fulfilling tree. Yet this is not the result of any action on his part, and he is not attached to any of it.

This morning, a family was telling me that once they had asked Baba if they could go into business with someone in Texas.

Baba had replied, "It doesn't sound like a good idea to me."

They told him, "Well, Baba, we've already done a lot of work on it. If we withdraw now, we wouldn't look good, and we would lose our future contracts."

Baba said, "I understand you, but it doesn't sound like a good idea to me."

They insisted: "Baba, please give us your blessings anyway."

Baba said, "It does not sound like a good idea to me."

They thought, "Well, we asked for blessings, so it will be all right."

They went ahead with the business, and in a week it fell apart because the partner stole all the money and ran away.

They came back to Baba and said, "Baba, you were right."

Baba asked, "What did you do?"

They said, "We went against what you said. We're sorry."

"You didn't go against me," Baba said. "You asked, and I told you. If you don't follow my advice, it doesn't mean you have gone against me."

This is the understanding of a great being. A great being's actions do not bear fruit in the sense that he is not disturbed by anything that happens. A lot of us would have said, "I told you! You should have listened to me! I always give good advice!" because we are attached to what we say and do. But for one who has understood the Truth, there is no more attachment to what is said and done. When one becomes free from attachment, one is able to live a good, clean, joyful life. Through practice and dispassion, you become established in the Truth.

> Not being associated any longer
>   with the bondage of birth,
> He reveals himself by the rays of the Self.
> He is the sun which is Shiva, the Lord.

A lot of people came to see Baba and felt so scared that they ran away. After a while they would come back and tell Baba, "I am very scared of you."

Baba would ask, "Why?"

Often they would reply, "Because when I came into your presence, my whole life flashed before my eyes."

This is a common saying. But what does this experience mean?

What passes before our eyes is not a great picture of our lives; rather, we experience the fear that comes from constantly running away from life. That is what passes before us.

Baba would say, "It is very good. It will go away."

Such people would come back even though they were scared. Then, when they really understood the answer to the question "What have I brought with me? What am I going to take back with me?" their fear would go away, and regardless of what place they were in, what time it was, or whom they were with, they would not be afraid.

Many people are afraid of the ocean; still, they go swimming. They go to the ocean and see the waves, and their heart beats wildly, but still they plunge into the water and swim. What do we fear? We fear death. We fear loss. When we say that our whole life flashed before our eyes, we are talking about our fear that someone will take away our friends and destroy what we have accumulated, that we will lose what we think we have. When we become established in the Truth, this fear dissolves like the salt doll in the ocean.

In the *Kulārnava Tantra* it is said:

Contemplation, even for a moment, of the truth
"I am the Truth, I am the Absolute"
Wipes out all sins,
Just as the rising sun dispels all darkness.

Forget about your fears. Let go of your bondage, of everything that you think strangles you. Free yourself from fear's noose and contemplate "I am that I am." The scriptures talk about the cave of the heart. Go to the cave of the heart.

This contemplation, which becomes a constant experience, wipes out all sins. We have a lot of ideas about what sins are and what our mistakes are. Sins are nothing but our fears. We commit sins because of fear. We make mistakes because of fear. Fear is the cause of everything that is unnecessary.

When we contemplate, when we have a constant experience of the Self, we are no longer afraid. When we are in that state in which there is no fear, we do not commit sins.

People often asked Baba, "Aren't you afraid?"

Baba would say, "No. I am not."

This was a reality. In Oakland, Baba went for daily walks. One time, two huge Dobermans came charging at him. The people walking with Baba were supposed to be protecting him, but when the dogs charged, two of them hid behind Baba's back. Baba just stopped and said, "Hello!"

The dogs were confused because they had never heard a "hello" from an Indian swami. They stood there and stared at him, and he looked back at them. Then, for no good reason, they turned around and went back to their house. Everyone breathed a sigh of relief and remembered their mantra. Baba didn't say anything. He just kept walking. He never said, "Oh, those people!"

For him the experience was nothing unusual. But when we see something that we think threatens us, our reaction is usually to run away or to fight. Fear takes over, and we act from that fear; we try to defend ourselves. But Baba knew that whatever was going to happen would happen. But then, Baba's faith was very strong.

Even a moment of contemplation can bring about strength and steadiness. When you experience this strength, love springs forth. Remember, Bholenath said, "Have you ever understood what love is all about?"

Everywhere we go, there is a lot of talk about love, yet at times we feel dry, we feel cheated; we feel we were not given enough love. Once again, we are attributing love to a person, place, or object. We always think it comes from something or someone out there. This is our idea of love. But, in his *Bhakti Sūtras*, the great sage Narada says, "Devotion is supreme love directed toward God." When we direct love toward God, then our love and devotion include everything.

A lot of people get scared when their friends or members of their family start loving God, because they feel that they will be excluded, but that is not the case. When you love God, everything and everyone is included, because the love of God contains everything. It is unselfish. When you live in that love, you can see the same love in ferocious animals and in docile ones, in those who hate you and in those who love you.

The sage Narada continues, "Devotion is supreme love directed toward God, and is not opposed to absorption in the Self." We are taught in Vedanta, "Have no attachment. Have no desire." Nevertheless, the scriptures say, "Have one attachment — to God. Have one desire — to attain God." This attachment is free from petty attachments. This desire is free from petty desires. Through this attachment, through this desire, we attain something great, something higher.

Shankaracharya says:

> Devotional love is the greatest of all means to liberation.
> Longing for meditation on the Self is called devotion.

Devotion or love does not mean just shaving your head and walking down the street screaming God's name. It is a constant experience, whether you are mopping the floor or taking a rocket to the moon. Without this experience, nothing really changes.

Over the centuries, a lot of leaders have tried to change the world. Some have tried to change it through guns, others through preaching, and still others by giving material goods. But the world can truly change only when each individual changes inside. If each individual does not change inside, trying to bring everyone under one roof is not easy, because opposing this effort there is a built-in mechanism — forgetfulness. People easily forget about good and evil. When there is this forgetfulness and you try to change things externally, that change stays on the surface; it does not seep in.

Supreme devotion is meditation on the inner Self, not on the body. It is the same as contemplating "I am that I am." When we have this higher understanding, we find real consolation in our lives. Otherwise, there is no contentment.

When I was in Hawaii, the incident of the *Challenger* space shuttle took place. I watched the whole program on the news. Again and again they showed the shuttle exploding in the air. The newspaper described it as "ironically beautiful," because as it exploded it formed the image of a swan.

Everyone was talking about it. Everyone worried that the children had been affected by it, but when they talked to them, they found the children really had a greater understanding. They looked at it from a much higher standpoint than we adults did.

Everyone wanted to know what would happen in the future and asked different questions. However, there was one particularly important moment when they asked a senator what would happen next. What would the politicians do? Would they let the program continue? How would the president explain all this to the astronauts' families, to the American people, and to the rest of the world?

The senator was very composed. He said, "We are always trying to look for answers outside. However, we cannot find the answers in any way from the outside, only from deep within."

It was beautiful that someone in that position could speak about something deep within. I am sure others must have thought that he was speaking in an inappropriate way. Yet he was bold and could speak the truth: "The answers have to be found deep within."

Who can explain this event? The astrologers said the shuttle did not lift off at an auspicious time: all the planets were in difficult aspects, and nobody had consulted them. The psychics said, "Well, these people were destined to have a spectacular death, so that they could be pioneers and could be reborn in a better human body." The engineers said, "Maybe we did not put the bolts in the right place." Other scientists pondered over what they might have done wrong. Family members grieved; they missed their loved ones and did not know what to do. Everyone was looking for the answer, looking for the truth.

Somehow there is no real explanation, even though all these people are trying their best to look for the truth and to put all the pieces together. Everyone did his best, and there is no real answer as to why such a thing happens. Why does anyone die? Why does anyone take birth? Why does anyone go anywhere?

The answer comes only when we enter the cave of the heart, when we become established in knowledge and experience the great love that arises when we attach ourselves to the Almighty. We do not have to try to make the Almighty into something other than what that Principle is. We have to accept the Principle as it is. We have to perform our duty, yet live in the experience of knowledge and love.

Narada says there are three kinds of devotion: one is *sattvic* devotion, a pure form of devotion. The second one is *rajasic* devotion, a mixture of pure and impure, which is for the sake of acquiring fame, worldly pleasures, and power. The third one is *tamasic* devotion, which is totally impure and is motivated by anger, hypocrisy, jealousy, and a desire to injure others.

You see these three types of devotion in different people, and to different degrees. People do have love and devotion, but for different reasons. Therefore Narada says, "Let your love be free of all this. Then you have attained great knowledge and great truth."

There was a wife who constantly nagged her husband. The husband said, "You told me you had forgiven and forgotten all my mistakes. Why do you keep bringing them up?"

She said, "I have to remind you because I don't want you to forget that I have forgiven and forgotten them."

42

There is always a catch in our love. We love everyone and every-thing, with a little condition: "I did this for you, so you should do this for me. I love you, so you should love me the same way." Narada says that this is not the purest form of love. In the purest form of love, you are absolutely free.

Bholenath says:

Where do we come from? Where are we going?
When you chew a betel nut, your mouth becomes red;
In the same way, when all the elements are combined,
    there is life in this body.
If you do not recognize what is beyond this body
    and deep within it,
You live in continuous ignorance.

The reason we do the practices is to transcend body consciousness, so that we can live happily in the body.

A lot of people ask for healing of the body, the mind, or the soul. You should understand that the soul never gets sick. Some people say, "My soul is possessed," or "My soul is wounded." However, the soul is very pure. It is beyond all the effects of this world. It is the mind which becomes sick or tied up when we have petty attachments.

Even for the healing of the body, we must get rid of petty attach-ments. Why do we have headaches, for example? Ninety-nine percent of the time, headaches occur because we worry so much, and we are so anxious. We must look for what is dissatisfying to us. The moment we understand it, we will become free of it.

"Where do we come from? Where do we go?" We come from the Truth and we go back to the Truth. "Where do we live in the meantime?" We live in the Truth and we will finally merge into the Truth, just as the salt doll merged into the ocean.

But we try to be very smart and clever. A man learned the language of the tigers. He talked to many, but they were all uninteresting. Finally he found the wisest tiger.

He approached him and asked, "What is mud?"

The tiger said, "Mud is sticky. And when it dries up, it tickles your paws."

The man asked, "What are bushes for?"

The tiger said, "Bushes help us to conceal ourselves from our enemies. And sometimes they get in the way of our whiskers."

The man thought, Oh well, I'll ask a question about human beings. And he said, "What is man's greatest disability?"

The tiger said, "Not having claws."

The man realized that tigers are basically uninteresting, no matter how wise they seem to be.

As the man walked away, a cheetah came up to the tiger and asked, "What was he talking about?"

"Oh," the tiger said. "He was just some stupid fellow asking stupid questions, so I gave him stupid answers."

We think that when we gain a little knowledge we can test someone very wise. But somehow we have not tested what kind of knowledge we ourselves have. It is very important to go deep within. We cannot get the answers even from the wisest tiger.

When we live on the surface of the mind and the intellect, we do not know their core. Why can't the mind easily understand the Truth? The Truth lives within the mind. Just as the body cannot know the light inside, so the mind finds it difficult to know the Truth. Why can't the intellect grasp the Truth immediately? The Truth lives within the intellect. The intellect is the body of the Truth. The only way to know the Truth is to merge with it completely.

There is no need to be afraid of losing body consciousness. Particularly among beginners, there is a lot of fear of losing one's identity. But there is a greater identity than the one you are afraid of losing, and that is the experience of "I am that I am." This experience is knowledge and love. Through it you can live with contentment, and you can also die peacefully.

When you rise above the fear of birth and death, you can live in the present regardless of how the past was, or of how the future will be.

Go deeper than the bones and the flesh. Experience this in the cave of the heart. And once you have the experience, it will flow through your bones and through your flesh. You will become walking knowledge, you will become living love. Rise above fear.

We will chant the mantra *Om Namah Shivāya.* Those of you who cannot let go of fear, put your fear into the sound. The sound will dissolve the fear. For the experience of knowledge and love, fear must dissolve — this is very important.

Let the chant resound throughout the body. Make sure that the sound reaches every pore. A lot of people think that singing means just having a sweet or beautiful voice. Chanting the mantra is not like that. It is focusing on the sound entering and being awakened in every pore of the body. So let the sound be awakened.

As this happens, we no longer feel uneasy whenever we sit for meditation. Often when we try to become quiet and still, we start asking, "How am I doing? What is going to happen?" We panic. But when we become still in the sound, we are at ease. And when we are completely at ease, we can have a tremendous experience of knowledge and devotion — unmixed devotion and crystal-clear knowledge. The freeing knowledge, the freeing love.

When you are sitting for meditation, if you do not know what to do, focus on the heart region. Start from there. There is a beautiful cave in the heart, very still and serene.

With great respect and with great love, I welcome you all with all my heart.

Sadgurunāth Mahārāj kī Jay!

Make Your Body
a Shrine for the Name

Oakland, California, February 9, 1986

WITH GREAT RESPECT AND LOVE, I welcome you all with all my heart. With the return of Halley's Comet over the last few months, there has been a lot of upheaval in everyone's life.

Many people do not understand the effects of the planets and stars, or of Nature in general. If you have not practiced self-inquiry, if you have not really gone deep inside, then it is very difficult to understand the way Nature influences your life. So if you are going through heavy times, just be patient and wait.

One of the main areas affected is that of relationships, whether between married couples or just people who like each other. Friends complain that they do not seem to get along. Married couples fight. Whatever the husband says annoys the wife, and whatever the wife says annoys the husband.

Some people think the easiest thing to do is to get a divorce, but that is no solution. And of course in the West, although now it is spreading everywhere, the idea is to find someone else. We always think, "This person is causing me pain. If I just give up this person, someone else will bring me joy."

For six months or for two years, it is fine, but then problems arise. So we keep getting divorced and remarried; we keep finding someone else. But that is not the ultimate solution. Baba said that when you go deep within, you realize that everyone is basically the same. Problems arise according to the times.

While Halley's Comet passes over, have patience and forbearance, and develop the strength to be tolerant. After this year it will be fine to make any decision you want, but do not make decisions when you are not clear, when the time is very difficult. At a time like this, it is best to go deep inside. Understanding your own Self is the best solution.

At the Intensive in Honolulu, a man from Los Angeles shared his experience. He said, "I had so much love for Gurumayi, but now it is fading." He went on and on, and, of course, everyone laughed. They thought it was very funny and cute; no one knew the story behind the story.

When I was in Los Angeles, I gave a lot of encouragement to this fellow because he seemed to need it. At the beginning of darshan, in the middle of darshan, and at the end of darshan, I looked at him, I spoke to him, and I listened to what he had to say.

When he came to Honolulu, it was time to stop that. You must not make someone dependent on external attention. If a person has not grown from what he has received, it is better to withdraw and make him a little stronger. So this time when he came up in the darshan line, I looked the other way. He waited and waited. He had brought a big gift, but I kept looking away. As he waited, everyone said to him, "Keep moving! You are blocking the darshan line."

He said, "No, no. Gurumayi knows me."

As it happened, that evening a lot of people wanted to speak to me. Finally he walked away.

He returned the next night. You can always sense such people. I made it a point not to look up, even though I knew he was there.

For three nights the same thing happened, and then he took the Intensive. During the Intensive I made sure of where he was sitting, so I would not look at him. But instead of understanding, "There must be a reason for this; I must learn something and grow from it," he got up and said, "I used to love Gurumayi so much, but now my love is fading."

I laughed and laughed. This is the story of everyone's life. If we receive outer attention, we think, "Ahh! My Guru loves me so much! God loves me so much. My wife or husband loves me so much. My child loves me so much."

True love is not based on outer attention. True love is an inner treasure which grows and grows. To experience it, go deep inside. If you do not get support from inside, no matter how much outer support you get, it is never going to be enough. You will always be flying from one flower to another, like a bee.

You have to know that the honey is inside, not just outside. But when you do get love from outside, drink it. Don't push it away. When we are given love, we say, "Perhaps I am not worthy of receiving this love. When I am deserving enough, I will take it." When love comes, experience it then and there. And when you think you are not getting love from outside, take it from inside. There is so much love within.

There is a saying, "Practice makes perfect." In Siddha Yoga, practice is necessary to become perfect. Even after you become perfect, practice is still worthwhile. Baba used to say that in the beginning *sādhanā* is the means, and at the end sadhana is the fruit. There was no reason for Baba to meditate after having attained realization, but he never stopped. At that point, meditation is not the means, but the fruit, and you relish it.

Most of us think of spirituality as worship, prayer, or invocation. That is fine. Worship makes us become one-pointed. So does prayer, and so does invocation. When we worship or pray, we are invoking the *Shakti*, and we are directly focusing on God's energy. However, there has to be someone to hold the energy that has been awakened through worship, prayer, or invocation. If you do not make yourself a vessel to hold it, then it all goes to waste. Meditation makes you a vessel strong enough to hold God's energy. Therefore it is said, meditation is worship, meditation is prayer, and meditation is invocation.

In these days meditation has become very fashionable. One meditates to lose weight, to look nice, or because everyone else is doing it. We have so many external concepts of what meditation is. Baba did not deny them, because whatever your concept of meditation, something still happens inside, and one day you do become aware of it.

But why wait for that day? Understand it now. Meditation is the essence of spirituality.

The moment we start talking about meditation, people remember their religion. "Do I have to give up Christianity?" "Do I have to give up Judaism?" "Do I have to give up Hinduism or Islam?" "I was brought up in this faith or that faith."

Meditation is the core of all religions. All religions sprang forth from the awareness of meditation, from the inner attainment. As time went on, people forgot the essence of each path or religion, and they got stuck in the externals. Now, when they want to return to the source, they feel confused and disloyal. But meditation is the core of everything and everyone. Just as sleep is necessary for the body, meditation is absolutely essential for the soul. Do you feel disloyal to your religion for sleeping?

Only in meditation do we feel complete satisfaction, complete contentment. Otherwise, we drink for intoxication, only to get a hangover later. We overeat because we want to feel high, only to get sick. We run around trying to find the Truth — only to feel exhausted. True intoxication comes when we live in the state of inner Truth, and when we take that same state into everything that we do, into every aspect of our lives.

Meditation, this amazing force, is both dynamic and subtle. Faith is good, but not blind faith. When you have experiences in meditation, you realize what faith is and what lack of faith is. As human beings, we are impressionable. This is a good quality, but we don't want to become gullible. We need to use our own inner understanding. For this we have to have a feeling of worthiness, and not base our understanding on the ego or past impressions. "Once burned, twice shy," they say — we don't want this kind of understanding.

We must have the feeling of worthiness — not that which comes from the sense of ego, but the purest form. If we do not feel worthy, we cannot think clearly. At times we might have inspiration, but it does not last. To feel worthy, we have to know what is within us. And to know what is inside, we have to have faith — not blind faith, but faith in meditation.

Meditation is the power to look within. Looking within does not mean turning the eyeballs outside in. Just as the senses have the tendency to go outward, they also have the ability to go inside. Just as the eyes can look outside, there are inner eyes which can look within. The senses can work both ways.

To live a balanced life, we need both the inner and the outer vision. We are amazed at psychics, astrologers, and others who have the power of looking into the future, knowing the past, and reading minds. But we are never amazed at the fact that every one of us has this potential.

Most of us are bored, but we are so lazy and our laziness is the reason for our boredom. Boredom can be very good. Why do you think Baba left his home when he was very young? He was bored — as simple as that — but he was a genius. His boredom was not "I don't know how to live this life," but "I *want* to know how to live this life. I *want* to know the Truth." And that led him to the ultimate realization. So boredom can be wonderful. It can take us to the Almighty; it can take us to the final goal.

The only way we can understand this is by looking within and experiencing it. To help us turn within, we will practice some techniques for the body and the mind, so that later on, no matter where we are or what we are doing, we can use these techniques to turn inside.

Many poet-saints have put their experience into song. Some wrote in a way everyone can understand, and some in a very mysterious way. Some gave just one word, and then left it up to the seeker to discover its meaning. But most saints were more compassionate; they told us more openly about their experience. One says:

> Remember the Name with great love.
> Just by doing this, you will become
>   free from worries.
> Remember the Name with great love.

We will chant the mantra, the Name: *Om Namah Shivāya*. Repeat it with love. Let down all your defenses. You can put them back up later. You do not need them now because you are just sitting and doing nothing. No one will enter your territory, so repeat the Name with love.

Become conscious of your body. Become conscious of it from head to toe. As you repeat the Name, install the sound of the Name in every pore. Let go of everything except one thing: love.

You can chant with your eyes closed or with your eyes open, but focus inside. When you repeat the Name, you are invoking the inner power. When you add love to the Name, the experience is even greater.

> The body that repeats the Name is a holy place.
> It becomes sacred.
> Such a body is virtuous.

The sages say that your body has to become the temple, the shrine, of the inner power. We have terrible feelings about our bodies. We always want to be someone else, someone we watch on TV or read about in magazines. Somehow we are not able to accept the temple that we have. This is because we have not established a connection with the inner power.

When there were no spaces left in the Intensive, some people said, "Can't you have an overflow room? You could use the breeze-way. We don't have to receive the touch. We just want to be there."

They were so sincere that I said, "All right. We have a small room in the back which can hold ten people. You can come and sit there."

Yesterday a new person in that room began to feel disconnected

51

even though he was right next door. And this is our life story: We have the temple of our body, but still we experience a feeling of disconnection. Many people say, "I have been away from the Guru for so long that I feel disconnected. I need to reconnect." We are disconnected from ourselves. If we are connected with ourselves, there is never a feeling of being disconnected from the Guru.

For the inner experience to take place, the body must become sacred and holy. The Name is a wonderful connection. Even though we use these syllables, it is actually the power of sound behind them which removes the barrier of the body, so that we can experience oneness inside and outside.

Having made the body a shrine for the power to dwell within, it is time to deal with the mind. The saint says:

Having made your body a shrine,
now sit very quietly.
Let the mind be completely empty
of all things.

When the body becomes a shrine and the mind empty of all its contents, there is complete purity. Then there is no end to joy and love.

When your body and mind are free of impressions and thoughts, your experience is completely transformed. A hollow stick of bamboo can create different sounds. If it is not hollow, the sound is not clear. Similarly, you need to empty yourself so that God's power can move about freely within and without. Then remain in this state. Another saint said:

Such stillness
Is like a motionless flame.
The sky remains unperturbed,
No matter how many clouds come and go.

Once you empty yourself of everything and become as pure as ether, then no matter what happens, your awareness is not destroyed.

A lotus in a muddy pond
Is not attached to the mud;
It lives there free from everything,
Beautiful and pure.

When you empty yourself of everything and make your body a shrine, you remain untouched by what goes on in this world. You remain beautiful; you remain clean.

When you merge into the Self, your true nature,
You remain joyful and happy.

Completely forget your body. Forget that you are sitting here, yet listen. Then do not even listen; let the words simply enter you. You have made your body a beautiful shrine, a sacred place.

The body is a lotus which has four petals: the physical, the subtle, the causal, and the supracausal. Many people complain about not having any experiences because they only remain in the first petal. Sometimes they go to the second petal, which is the dream state.

The most wonderful experiences arise from deep within, like a volcanic eruption. We have many layers. We are always boiling underneath with light and heat, but we deal only with the hard outer crust. For this reason, we are not able to experience anything greater than the hardness of our outer being. In meditation, we pass through these hard outer layers, the hard petals. Through the power of sound, we are able to go inside. Sound is a great vehicle.

The subtle body, which is as big as the thumb, is a white light. The causal body is the size of a fingertip, and it is dark. The supracausal body is a tiny blue dot. From this tiny blue dot, everything springs forth. It is the seed of the universe, the seed of our life. To understand and experience this blue dot, which is smaller than the smallest, we need the finest intellect, with no hard layer covering it; it has to be very, very fine. Keep going deeper and deeper inside. Do not set a time limit for yourself. Do not think, "Now or never."

Even though there is a tremendous amount of grace in our lives, still we need to acknowledge it. Meditation is a way of showing our gratitude for what God has placed inside us, as well as for what we have received on the outside. If we do not give ourselves this time, we become restless. The soul needs its own time.

Many people think meditation happens in only one way, but there are many ways. The body is not an obstacle. When you first learn to meditate, you sit in a particular posture and keep your body straight. However, as you continue to meditate every day, you can sit in different postures. There are different stages and phases in meditation. You cannot always sit with your back straight. When you meditate at home you can rest your back against a wall. Sometimes when you sit for meditation, the head drops forward. Just take a pillow and rest your forehead on that. During meditation, allow the body to position itself however it wishes. The awakened energy wants the vessel to be a certain way so that it can do its work. Allow that to happen; don't be rigid.

Keep your mind as still as a flame in a windless place. Empty the body of all its dross, so it can feel very light.

Tukaram Maharaj said:

> This blue dot is smaller than the smallest,
> Yet brighter than the brightest.
> It is the light of all lights.

We must go very deep inside in meditation to have the vision of this light. Then we can carry this light as our perception and see everything through it. Otherwise, we wear different veils and see the world through them, and we are not able to see the world as it is, or to accept it as it is.

The great saint Ramdas was singing the glories of Lord Rama and describing a beautiful flower in Sri Lanka. He said, "This flower is white. It grows only in heaven, but because of the Lord's presence in Sri Lanka, it also grows there. It is soft and delicate, and its fragrance is divine." Of course, everyone was becoming intoxicated just listening to the description of this beautiful white flower.

Hanuman, the Lord of the Monkeys, was present, listening to Ramdas sing the glories of Lord Rama. He had been to Sri Lanka on an errand. However, while he was there he was very angry, because he had come to rescue Sita from the hands of a demon called Ravana. Hanuman had seen this flower, and he burst out immediately, "That flower is not white! It is red!"

Ramdas had not been to Sri Lanka, but he had had a vision of this beautiful flower. He said, "It is white. I saw it inside, and that cannot be wrong."

Hanuman said, "But I was there, and I actually saw it. It was red!"

Ramdas replied. "No, my inner experience cannot mislead me."

Hanuman said, "Are you calling me a liar? I saw it with my own eyes. How can you say that I am wrong? It is red — not white!"

Ramdas explained: "Hanuman, you were so angry that your eyes were bloodshot, so you saw it as red, but it is white."

We need the inner eye, which people call the third eye, so that we do not look at things through the perspective of our emotions, our grudges, our foolishness, or our ego. We need it so that we can value and evaluate every situation through the inner understanding and the inner perception.

When we see the inner light, it envelops our entire being. It cleanses the mind, the intellect, and the ego; it cleanses the shrine of the body until it becomes more and more worthy of holding the power of God.

Tukaram Maharaj says:

When I pierced through all the three bodies —
   physical, subtle, and causal —
I saw the light inside.
When I went beyond the mind, the intellect,
   and the ego,
I saw the light inside.
Now I am able to see the same light
In all three bodies and in all the instruments —
   the mind, intellect, and ego.

Even though you are listening to something outside, do not lose your inner focus. Strength comes from deep within, from the sense of worthiness, the sense of greatness, and the inner experience.

When you experience the light within, it makes everything very clear. When we understand something in our day-to-day life, we say, "It dawned on me." A bolt of light hits us, and we experience insight. Some of us call it love, some of us call it knowledge, and some of us call it revelation.

Usually we feel, "Oh, I will have to climb mountains and cross oceans to find the Truth!" But when we see the light, we realize we will not need to overcome big obstacles — just small ones.

A great saint, Ibrahim, had a needle in his hand. It slipped out of his fingers and fell into a lake. Ibrahim sewed clothes to make a living. It was the only needle he had, and he was very poor. He looked into the lake and called, "O fish! Could one of you please find my needle!"

He had a great connection with Nature and had realized the Truth in every being. Hundreds of thousands of fish came out of the water, each one with a diamond needle in its mouth. Ibrahim looked at them and said, "None of these is my needle."

They all dived down and came up again with hundreds of thousands of golden needles. Ibrahim said, "None of them is my needle."

Again they dived, and this time they came up with silver needles.

Ibrahim sat down and said, "None of them is mine."

Finally one little fish stuck its head out of the water with Ibrahim's needle in its mouth. "That's the one!" he said, and he took it.

A lot of us would have wanted the other needles, but Ibrahim did not. When you become very pure and clean, every little bit of greed and carelessness vanishes. You are totally one-pointed on your duty, on what you need. When there is absolute clarity, you realize there is no need to perform great or miraculous feats. You just perform your duty, however simple.

The other day someone asked me, "Why is the Truth so simple?" But that is just how it is: the Truth is simple and easy. Once you have the experience of the light, the Truth within, you can still have your crazy mind, but you can play with it. You can still have everything that you have always had, but with clarity.

People have the fear that they will lose their identity if they merge into the Truth, but the identity which they are afraid of losing is false. Once you merge into the Truth, you can use that old false identity to make others gain a greater understanding of what they are. Everything that we have, we can use as a vehicle. When we see through the inner light, there is complete clarity, complete purity. Even when we feel we are in a mess, we can see our life changing like patterns of oil on the water. We do not feel that we are ruined. We can grow from each calamity. It is so important to have this experience of knowing that the mind and the senses do not limit us.

There is a scientist who is also a devotee of Baba's. He spends every summer in South Fallsburg, but this year, just before he was going to leave his home, he was offered a big job involving more than a million dollars. He was in a dilemma: Should he go to Fallsburg or take the job? He thought about it. It was either the inner experience or the job. Every year he had gone to Fallsburg, so he turned down the offer.

He went to Fallsburg, and every now and then his mind ate him up: "You could have had so much. . . . " But he had heard many talks about greed and lack of faith, so he stuck to his decision. When he went back after a month, there was another offer waiting — this one for five million.

Now this is a very simple story. There is nothing much to it if you say, "Oh, it was just a matter of luck." Yet it involves something very profound. To have as much faith as that, you have to have understanding; you have to have gone beyond the hard outer layer. Then you have the ability to accept anything and everything. Once you go beyond everything and have the complete experience of the Truth, life has a different meaning. Tukaram Maharaj says:

> Now I live only for the sake of humanity,
> Just to help.

You are no longer living to serve your body; you are living to serve the Truth. When this shift takes place, life has a greater meaning.

The reason we are bored in our lazy way, the reason we become nonchalant, the reason we have no love for other people, is that we are only serving our own body. Everything that we do is to please the eyes, the ears, the nose, the tongue, the hands, and the legs. We love someone else so that they can please our body. We obtain something else so that it can please our body. It is complete selfishness. We do not experience true joy, because everything is "for me, for me, for me." And it is not for the real "I" inside, either, but just for the hard outer cover. Nothing can satisfy the hard cover except the senses.

When the inner experience takes place, everything shifts. You want to live because your life brings about great happiness for others. You are not eaten up by greed, by desire, by anger, or negativity because you are no longer serving them. You are serving the higher Truth, the real purpose of life.

Then, whether you are among people or all by yourself, the experience is the same. It is not that when you are with people you feel wonderful and when you are all by yourself you feel like a worm, or vice versa. It does not matter whether you are with people or all alone. You always experience a connection, because you have merged into the Truth.

With great respect and with great love, I welcome you all with all my heart.

Sadgurunāth Mahārāj kī Jay!

Valentine's: A Day of Love

Mexico City, February 14, 1986

WITH GREAT RESPECT AND LOVE, I welcome you all with all my heart. You can speak for hours about love. But in the end, one question still remains: What is love?

Love is indescribable. No matter how much love is expressed, there is always a little bit more. And what we want is that "little bit" that has not yet been expressed. No matter how much love and affection we get, there is still a feeling of emptiness inside. That space can be filled only through the inner experience of love. And this love is God, the Truth.

Without the experience of love, everything else is meaningless. No matter how many beautiful things we see, how many beautiful houses we have, how many beautiful clothes we own, or how many beautiful people are around us, there is still emptiness. Everything that we do, we do for love. But the river has to merge into the ocean to attain perfection. Without the experience of merging, no matter how many philosophies we read or spiritual practices we perform, there is no attainment. Some people say, "I do not believe in all this." The great author Dostoyevsky said:

> Love all God's creation, both the whole and every grain of sand. Love every leaf, every ray of light. Love the animals, love the plants, love each separate thing. If you love each thing, you will perceive the mystery of God in all. And when once you perceive this, you will thenceforward grow every day to a fuller understanding of it, until you come at last to love the whole world, with a love that is all-embracing and universal.

Once we experience this all-embracing, universal love, we can believe in it. When we go to the ocean with a little cup, we will only get a little water. If we have a bigger container, we will get more. If we have a bucket, we will get still more. How much we get depends upon the size of the container that we carry.

A saint said:

> O Lord, what do You lack in Your court?
> You have so much to offer.
> What can I do?
> The bag of my heart is so small.

Baba taught Siddha Yoga for many years, and he gave himself completely to what he taught. Over the years, people have come and have received whatever they have been able to carry. A doctor said, "Baba knows medicine very well." An engineer said, "He is a very good engineer." A psychotherapist said, "He is a very good psychotherapist." A businessman said, "He is a very good businessman." A student said, "He is a very good listener." A monk said, "He is a very good monk." A teacher said, "He is a great teacher." All the people who came took away what their understanding allowed them to take. But a true seeker lost himself or herself in Baba completely, like a river merging into an ocean. Love is this total absorption. Without it, love is not really love; it is affection, attachment, or giving favors.

But if love is so obvious, why is it so hidden?

There was a smuggler called Nasrudin. Every day he crossed the border to Mexico with a donkey carrying hay. Although the customs officer inspected his load every day, he could not find what Nasrudin was smuggling. For thirty years Nasrudin crossed the border daily, and he never got caught. Then both he and the customs officer retired, and they became neighbors.

One day as Nasrudin was washing his donkey, the former customs officer looked over the fence and asked him, "Tell me, what were you smuggling all those years?" But Nasrudin was not willing to give out the information so easily.

The ex-officer coaxed him: "Look, I won't tell anyone. It doesn't matter now. You're retired and I'm retired. Please tell me, Nasrudin. I *know* you were smuggling."

Nasrudin finally said, "All right, officer, if you really want to know, I was smuggling donkeys."

So obvious, yet so hidden. This is how it is with love, with the inner experience. If we want it, it is there. If we do not look for it in the right place, thirty years may roll by and we will not find it. It is so obvious, yet so hidden.

No matter where we go, we have programs which are open to everyone night after night. Yet people come up and ask for Shaktipat. What do you think the program is for? Just so that I can enjoy looking at you? It is so obvious, yet so hidden.

This is why the sages never had to hide the Truth. God never had to hide the Truth. As human beings, we know how to miss everything.

People put blinders on a horse so it can see where it is going but does not get sidetracked, and for us, the practices are like this. The practices help us to become focused. Whenever there is a focus, the arrow goes straight to the mark. It has a lot more force and energy, and the experience is deeper and greater. We need this focus in order to have the feeling of love at all times.

A German poet said, "To love is good, although love is difficult. For one human being to love another is very difficult. That is, perhaps, the most difficult of all our tasks — the ultimate, the last test and proof, the work for which all other work is but preparation."

Our life's work is a preparation for the experience of love. Without this experience of love, we are dead while living, and everything around us also dies. Plants, trees, animals, birds, other people — everything dies from this lack of love. Inside us, all our cells die, never to be reborn. As each cell in the body dies, we no longer have a desire to live. When we give up on life, we become mean and cruel to other people, wanting to destroy everyone else's life.

When there is total absorption, however, there is love, and love creates life. It is very easy to experience love if we know how to be in every situation.

Once two birds saw a turtle. There wasn't enough water where the turtle was, so the birds felt compassion for him. They asked the turtle if he would like to go somewhere where there was more water.

He said, "Of course I would, but look at me. I move so slowly."

"That is fine," said the birds. "We can carry you. But do you know how to keep your mouth closed?"

The turtle exclaimed, "What a question!"

The birds said, "No, no, it is very important. You must answer. Do you know how to keep your mouth closed?"

"I do," said the turtle.

They brought a stick and asked him to clench it between his teeth. Then, taking both ends of the stick, they flew over different villages, towns, and cities.

Some children playing below saw them and cried out, "Oh, look at the turtle! He is flying with the birds!"

The turtle exclaimed, "What!?" and he plummeted to the earth.

We are like the turtle. We go to a Master and say, "Shaktipat! Initiation! Give me the experience." When the Master does not acknowledge us we get carried away and say, "I drove for so long to come here. I gave up everything. What was it all for?"

A great saint said, "O Lord, I have sent millions of letters to You. I have not received any answers. But I know *that* is Your reply."

When you have love, there is complete attainment. Initiation is not given by saying, "I will now give you initiation." Love is not awakened by saying, "I will now give you love." It is an inner happening, beyond the reach of the physical senses. The eyes do not know, the nose does not know, the mouth, the ears, and the hands do not know. But something happens, and they are all transformed. This is the nature of initiation, of inner absorption. For this reason, no matter how many doubts and negativities arise, no matter how much nonbelief there is, the inner happening takes place.

Once someone said to me, "I do not believe in God. Do you think He will still love me?"

I said, "It is very possible."

If God were to wait until we believed in Him, He would have to wait for many, many centuries. It takes a long time for us to cultivate faith and belief. I feel the most gratitude toward God when I remember that His love for us does not depend on our faith and belief. It is an inner happening. Once we have experienced this inner happening, it is good to keep cultivating it so that we can keep this love alive within us all the time.

There was a king who kept a vigil every night. His minister said to him, "O King, you work so hard all day long. Why do you need to pray to God at night?"

The king said, "Don't you know? All day God runs after me, but at night I pursue Him."

Many of us feel that since we have blessings and grace, we don't need to do anything. In a way, this is true, but we need to nurture our experience in order to keep it alive. Otherwise, since we are human, we know how to forget.

To live in the continuous experience of love, we need to keep focused and not get distracted. Baba Muktananda was able to give the teachings day after day because that was his focus. When there is this focus, it makes you greater and greater. People often ask for a bigger heart. For this great heart, you need a focus. You must choose your focus. Whatever that focus is, it will make you great.

Once a beggar went to a king to ask for something. As he was telling the king his problems, the iron rod that he carried dug into the king's foot. The beggar was unaware that the king's foot was bleeding. After he had told him all about his problems and the king had given him a gift of money, he left.

Afterward, while they were bandaging the king's foot, the minister asked him, "O King, why did you let him do this to you?"

The king said, "He came to me with his problems. He already had enough to bear. There was no need for me to tell him about the problem with my foot."

This is called a great heart. With a lot of us, if someone comes to tell us his problems, we say, "Listen to mine first." We behave in this way because we have no focus, no commitment. We do not know what we are doing. But the king knew what he was doing: He was ruling his subjects and giving his life to them. He had a focus. Therefore, he had a greater heart; he could embrace all of them. If you have a focus, you also attain the all-embracing love.

Yesterday, a young woman came up in the darshan line and said, "Gurumayi, my mother does not like me to come here. She doesn't believe in Siddha Yoga, and she doesn't like meditation or the idea of the Guru."

I said, "Let her know that when you come here you feel more love for her."

She said, "Ahh!"

This is what everyone wants: love. They are not opposed to your meditating. They are afraid that if you come here, you will forget them. When someone is against us, we see only the superficial reasons, but there is something else behind all that.

We need to eliminate this kind of conflict, and the only way we can do it is by experiencing love. Otherwise, a relationship becomes like a battle: You have your shield, and he has his shield. You have your sword, and he has his sword. You hit his shield, and he hits your shield. There is a great uproar and everyone says, "My God, a fierce battle is raging." But if we just drop our shields, then the only thing left is God's love, the tenderness behind the shield, the presence of the Almighty.

Once a person asked me, "Are you God, or am I God?"

I said, "God is inside me, and God is inside you."

She asked, "God is inside me also?"

I said, "That has been my experience: God is inside you, too."

Then tears came to her eyes. When you drop the shield of your concepts, there is only one thing left: the presence of God.

The Sufi *Book of Wisdom* says: "Nothing benefits the heart more than a spiritual retreat, wherein it enters the domain of meditation." Even though it seems we are not doing anything when we sit for meditation, a lot is happening inside. Even though it does not seem much like social work in the beginning, this transformation of the individual is actually the highest form of social work. When each individual carries his transformation to where he lives and works, he does a great service to humanity.

Let us make a pledge that, if not all day or all night long, at least for a few moments every day, we will make an effort to experience love, love that is free from selfishness, free from desire, free from expectation, love that is complete freedom. Just as the sky stays in its own place without any support, love must rest in itself without any support. That is true love.

When we repeat God's name, it awakens the inner love. When we sit for meditation in complete stillness, we are able to perceive the inner light. We can see it coursing through every vein of our body. The reason we cannot experience love and light all the time is that they are so fine, so subtle. As we ourselves become finer and finer, we, too, experience this inner love and light.

> With your mind completely transformed into love,
> Repeat the name of God,
> Repeat the name of the Lord.
> The power of the Name, along with your love,
> Will remove all your sins and miseries.
> You will cross over this world.

Repeat the mantra with your entire being. *Om Namah Shivāya.* Let the sound permeate you from head to toe. As you allow the body to absorb the sound, it is no longer just sound, but the nectar of love. This nectar of love is the real medicine for the body, the real therapy for the mind. When you experience the nectar of love, life in this world has meaning.

Namah Shivāya simply means "I bow to the Lord within." No matter how many difficulties we experience, no matter how many great times we have, let us not forget the inner love.

Last night you were asked to contemplate "Who am I?" Tonight, wait for the answer in the stillness of your meditation. It is real. Do not take it lightly. *Om Namah Shivāya.* Do it with your entire being. Make the sound come out of you very sweetly. It is good for the lungs, so don't cheat. If you want the fullness and richness of it, do it fully. *Om Namah Shivāya.* Let the sound come out of your body so that your whole being blossoms like a flower in the sound. Instead of walking around unconsciously, walk like a flower, listening to the inner music.

With great love and with great respect, I welcome you all with all my heart. Love is love. Respect is love. The heart is also love — and so are you.

Sadgurunāth Mahārāj kī Jay!

The Ego of Civilization

Mexico City, February 15, 1986

WITH GREAT RESPECT AND LOVE, I welcome you all with all my heart. Here, we get drunk on chanting, we get high on meditation, we attain contentment through our service. And everyone wonders, "How can this happen?"

A reporter once entitled his article on Baba "The Swami Is Drunk on Love." For just a moment Baba had looked into his eyes, and he had felt that intoxication. Why do we need the help of a Master to have this experience? Why do we need the support of the scriptures? The sages who had the experience say that the Truth is beyond the eyes, beyond the ears, beyond all the senses. For this reason, we need a vehicle other than the senses to experience the Truth. This vehicle is grace, which is God's compassion, His mercy. It is an inner happening, but when we experience the Truth through grace, the eyes see it and the ears hear it. When that grace flows through all our senses, then there arises the Absolute Knowledge, about which Shaivism speaks.

> Then you see this entire world
>   as a play of Consciousness.
> You are not bound by anything that happens.
> You are liberated while living.

The experience of the Truth, the attainment of liberation, does not come after we die but while we are living. For this incredible experience of liberation and the Truth, we maintain discipline.

In these days we think we are very civilized, but we are not civilized at all. We cannot sleep without taking pills. The air is so bad we cannot breathe without taking oxygen. We cannot talk to anyone without feeling embarrassed. We cannot sit in one place for more than ten minutes. We eat food, and then we take Alka-Seltzer. There is no discipline in this body. And we think we are so civilized!

We think we are "Westernized." "I am Westernized, so I don't believe in God." "I am Westernized, so I don't meditate." In the East, in the West, in the North, and in the South too, people say they are Westernized! Because they are Westernized, they wear pants that are so tight they can hardly sit down. But there is such restlessness! The mind is wandering. The stomach is growling. The ears want to hear everything except what they are hearing. The eyes want to see everything except what they are seeing. There is no peace — but there *is* the ego of "civilization."

It is because of this civilized ego that it is so hard to experience happiness in our own being, to experience the Truth.

Once there was a man who heard that he could attain supernatural powers by performing a certain practice, so he did that for years on end. Twenty-five years later he had attained the power to multiply himself into forty identical forms. He was thrilled. His ego was happy. He went from place to place performing this trick, and everyone said, "What a miracle!" This only encouraged him, and he kept multiplying himself into those forty identical forms.

Baba used to say that no matter how much ego you have, no matter how civilized you are, there is still one thing in life that you cannot avoid, and that is death. Death does not care what a great yogi or what a great householder you are. Death does not care what profession you have. Death does not care how sweetly or how badly you speak. Death has equal vision.

This man's day finally came. Because of his practices, he knew that the hour was approaching, and he got ready. When he heard the bells of the messenger of death, he multiplied himself into forty identical forms.

The messenger just stood there. He was supposed to take one man, but here were forty men who all looked the same. He was confused. He went back to the god of death and told him, "There were forty men. What could I do?"

The god of death knows human beings very well. He called another messenger and whispered into his ear, "Praise him! Praise him to death!"

This messenger went to the man, who again multiplied himself into forty forms. The messenger began to walk up and down, saying,

"Splendid! You are a great man. You are wonderful. You are handsome. You are incredible. There is nobody like you. You are the best! The highest! You have surpassed God in your powers of creation!"

As the adjectives got more and more superlative, the balloon of his ego kept getting bigger and bigger, and all the forty heads swelled up. The man was totally intoxicated with the praises of his feat.

Finally the messenger of death said, "But there is just one tiny mistake."

The real person jumped forward and shouted, "What's that?" The messenger of death put the rope around his neck and dragged him away.

We think death is this or that, but it is the ego that is the cause of our death. Whether you are a monk or a householder, a small person or a big person, it is the ego that becomes the cause of your death. Death is fine if it is death in the sense of leaving this world, but you die over and over while you are living. The sages say that if you have not experienced the Truth, your life is nothing but death.

The ego is so great that it prevents us from knowing what we really are. It does not allow us to turn within. However, we must make an effort.

Especially here, people have said to me, "The world needs peace; it is in a terrible condition." I wonder why it never occurs to us that if we become peaceful, our peace can spread. We never understand the fact that peace must start within ourselves.

What is the world? The mountains and the oceans and the trees? If that were the world, ah! wonderful! But people make the world.

One person thinks he needs peace, and then he thinks, "No. That man needs peace and that woman needs peace, and so does that person and that person." Meanwhile these people are thinking the same about him. People living in Durango think people in Guadalajara need peace, and people living in Guadalajara think the same about people living in Durango. Both think the people who are living in Mexico City need peace. Mexicans think the Africans need peace, Africans think the North Americans need peace, North Americans think the Indians need peace, Indians think the Europeans need peace. Everyone is thinking about it but no one is doing anything.

While living, we are dead. The civilized ego does not allow us to go inside ourselves and perceive the Truth. For this reason, we have to make an effort to go within. In the beginning meditation is an effort; at the end, meditation is the fruit of our effort.

In a *bhajan* the Lord is implored:

O Lord, give me one spark,
I ask only for one spark.
I have spent my whole life in ego,
   in desires, in greed;
I have been wallowing in all these things.
I have wasted my whole life.
There is no light in my body,
There is no light in my life.
O Lord, give me one spark, just one spark,
So that I can be lit once again.

It takes a lot to pray sincerely. We have prayed many times, but it is always "Give me this" and "Give me that." A true seeker prays for the highest, for one thing, one spark, so that his entire being can be lit. For this reason we do the practices continuously, day after day, night after night. These practices wipe away the hard edges of the ego and the emotions, and they brighten the intellect. Just as you polish gold, in the same way, these practices polish you.

In a great scripture called the *Yoga Vāsishtha*, the sage says:

Knowledge of the Truth is the fire
That burns all hopes and desires
As if they were dried blades of grass.

Meditation is not simply remaining quiet. "Knowledge of the Truth is fire." The sages always refer to spiritual experience as fire, light, a spark. People think that if you are on the spiritual path, you become dull, stupid, an idiot. But idiots do not last long on the spiritual path. The practices are too strong for them, and they fall away like dry leaves.

When the intellect is brightened, you perceive the Truth. Light is everywhere. However, it is reflected only in a clean mirror. When the heart is clean, the light of God is reflected very clearly. This reflection of light is not for someone else to look at and say, "Oh look, here comes the saint." It is for your own everyday experience of life.

The sage Vasishtha says:

On the field of the mind
The seed of meditation falls of its own accord,
When one is alone in the forest of wisdom.

The "forest of wisdom" is contemplation. Sometimes people ask, "How can I contemplate the Truth when I do not know what the Truth is?" Everything in this creation is the Truth. Contemplate a flower, and you will transcend the flower and see the light in the flower. Concentrate on the carpet and you will transcend the carpet and see the Truth in it. Contemplate your loved one and you will transcend flesh and bones and see the light in your beloved.

Once a farmer went to a great saint. Just as this evening, a discourse was going on. At the end, the farmer said to the saint, "I don't know what God looks like. I don't know how to meditate. What should I do? I really want to know the Truth."

The saint asked him, "What do you love the most?"

The farmer said, "My goat."

The saint said, "Very good. Go home and meditate on your goat." The farmer was delighted. He went back home, prepared a place for his meditation, sat on a pillow, closed his eyes, and began to think about his goat — its eyes, its horns, its tail. Every day as he meditated on his goat he became happier and happier. One day, as he started meditating, the room was filled with white light. The light was both inside and outside. His entire being became transparent.

It is said over and over again, contemplate what you like. Through this practice you will transcend the object and be able to see the Truth in it. This experience is possible in our day-to-day life. But we prefer to have the civilized ego.

"In the forest of wisdom," contemplate the Truth. The mind is like a field. Whatever you sow in this field is what will grow there. If you sow the seed of anger, anger will grow. If you sow the seed of love, love will grow. If you sow the seed of jealousy, jealousy will grow. If you plant the seeds of contemplation and love for God, they will grow in the field of the mind, and your being will be transformed.

The sage Vasishtha continues:

> Knowledge does not have any object;
> It is independent and eternal.
> It is beyond description and definition.
> When this truth is directly realized,
> There is perfect knowledge.

Knowledge of the Truth is independent of everything and everyone. Therefore, it is simply called "the experience." As long as we just live in the physical senses, we have limitations, but as we go deeper and deeper inside through contemplation and the power of sound, we cross the barriers of our limitations.

In ancient times, rather than constantly stealing from nature, people performed rituals in which they offered everything back to nature. Dust back to dust. God back to God. Once a monk was performing ritual offerings on the bank of a river. He took a little water in his hand and mentally offered it to God. However, there was a scorpion in the water, and it stung his hand. The monk took another handful of water, and the scorpion stung him again. He threw the water back into the river and took more. This kept happening again and again.

A spectator was watching this whole game. It does not matter what world you live in, you always have an observer. Whether you lead a household life or the life of a monk, there is always a witness. Finally he asked the monk, "If the scorpion keeps stinging you again and again, why don't you kill it?"

The monk said, "Listen. The nature of the scorpion is to sting. The nature I have cultivated is love. If a small creature like a scorpion does not give up its nature, should I, as a monk, give up mine?"

This is the sign of true peace. With us, experiences of peace last only as long as there is outer peace. When there is conflict, we get involved in it. This happens because we are "civilized." I am not condemning any particular civilization — do not misunderstand me. What is not good is the *ego* of civilization. Because of the ego of civilization, we are not able to live in harmony. If we just drop the ego, then no matter what happens, there is harmony. Then we are not greedy or envious, and we can do our duty without being greedy. For this state of complete harmony, we have to go beyond the physical senses. For complete peace, we have to have an inner experience. Without the inner experience, we feel that nothing is possible.

At the beginning of the tour we were in Japan. In Japan they are very civilized, but their civilization lacks one thing: ego. At the evening programs, I spoke for a long time with translation, just as I am doing here. No one coughed. No one sneezed. No one moved. It was an amazing experience. I wondered if God had placed statues in the hall. They were so still and so steady — and they were happy.

When they came up for *darshan*, it was the same. Every movement was graceful, and they asked for nothing. When they came to the Intensive, the hall monitors did not have to do any work. Without having to be told anything, people behaved as if they had practiced Siddha Yoga for centuries. They came in and sat themselves in rows; it was breathtaking. And when the time for meditation came, everyone went inside. I was absolutely astonished; I had never seen people like that before. And their experiences were incredible.

From where does this ability come? It comes from discipline alone — discipline without ego, without rigidity. I was there for a week. The night I was leaving, they had tears in their eyes — there was quite an outpouring of water. So it was not that they were unfeeling; they were not stony-hearted. When you already have this discipline without rigidity, the inner experience becomes possible right away. All you need is one phrase, *Tat tvam asi,* "Thou art That," and you have the experience, "I am the Truth." You hear, *Aham Brahmāsmi,* "I am the Absolute," and you have that experience.

When you are ready, when the field of the mind is properly cultivated, then you have to repeat the mantra only once and you are transformed, never to change again from the Truth.

There was a disciple who had been studying under a sage for many years. One day while the Master was out, a man brought his little child who was dead. The disciple thought, "This is the time to see if the power of the mantra works." So he took a bowl of water, repeated the mantra three times, and sprinkled the water on the child, who came back to life. The disciple was delighted; the father was overjoyed. He took his child home.

When the Master came back, the disciple could not wait to tell him the whole story. The Master got very angry. The disciple was really confused: It was such a great feat, yet the Master was upset.

He asked the Master, "Please explain to me why you are so distressed. Aren't you happy that the child came back to life?"

The Master said, "That is not the point. I am sad that your belief in the mantra is so small. Why did you repeat it three times? Once would have been enough!"

This is the truth. Baba said over and over again that when you are completely ready, one word carries the power of all the mantras. The mantra can be considered like a vacuum cleaner that sucks up all the impurities of the mind and leaves it spotless. The syllables that we repeat here are charged with the awakened energy of the great Masters.

We are here for the inner experience. The sages say that you do not attain the Truth merely through a lecture or through an intellectual discourse; you attain the Truth from within. So tonight we will chant the mantra that was repeated by the great sages of Maharashtra: *Jay Jay Vitthal, Jaya Hari Vitthal*. The meaning is very simple, as the Truth always is: "I hail the Lord; I hail the Lord." *Jay Jay* means "Hail, hail." And *Hari* and *Vitthal* are two different names of the same Lord. The literal meaning of the word *Hari* is "the one who takes away the fluctuations of the mind." And *Vitthal* means "the Lord who is firmly established within me."

The sound is God, Truth, and love. We must awaken the right sound within through the practice of chanting and prayer. So join in. If you find it difficult, then listen, because the sound can enter through the ears and through the pores of your body and awaken the energy inside.

Surrender to what you are doing. Relax with the awareness that this is the best thing you could be doing at this moment. When you become completely engrossed in what you are doing, you obtain the full fruit of it. Listen to the sound, or sing the sound. Do not just sing with your throat, but with your entire being. Afterward we will sit very quietly. Several nights ago we contemplated, "Who am I?" Last night we waited for the answer, and some people in the darshan line told me about their experiences, which were wonderful. Tonight, let us have the experience, "I am the Truth." Let everything turn inside, and then when it turns outside again, it will be very beautiful.

With great respect and with great love, I welcome you all with all my heart.

Sadgurunāth Mahārāj kī Jay!

Kundalini: The Awakening

Mexico City, February 16, 1986

WITH GREAT RESPECT AND LOVE, I welcome you all with all my heart. Last night someone gave me a little Mexican statue, and on its head was a snake. In every country, on every path, the image of *kundalinī*, the serpent power, is found.

The *Yoga Vāsishtha* explains why the supreme power is known as Kundalini:

> It is called Kundalini
> Because it is coiled in appearance.
> It is the supreme power,
> The prime mover of all beings.

In its coiled form, the supreme power lies at the base of the spine, which is the foundation of the entire system. In an ordinary person, this force is present, but it is dormant. It is awakened through initiation. You can always tell the difference between a person who is initiated and one who is not. In a person who is initiated, the light is awakened, and a splendor shines throughout the body, the mind, and the intellect. When this force is not awakened, there is no light of *viveka*, of discrimination. From a superficial standpoint, all that "viveka" means is knowing right from wrong, good from evil. However, from the highest standpoint, viveka is the awareness that all is one.

It is so hard for people to understand that there is something great inside them. It is very easy to think it is outside — in the mountains, in the caves, in the ocean. But inside? No!

Baba often told a wonderful story about an old woman who was sewing her clothes. She dropped her needle, so she immediately began to look for it by the light of a streetlamp. A friend of hers was passing by and asked her what she was doing.

She said, "I am looking for my needle."

Her friend also started looking for the needle. An hour passed by, but neither of them could find it. Finally the friend asked her, "Where did you lose it?"

"In the house," she said.

"Then why are we looking for it outside?"

"Because there is no light inside; the only light is out here."

Baba used to say that we are no different from that old woman. We look for everything outside because that is the only place we think we can see. But, though dormant, the force is inside; it must be awakened from within.

In the *Hatha Yoga Pradīpikā* it is said:

> The great Goddess Kundalini sleeps,
> Closing with Her mouth the opening
> Through which one can ascend
> To the *brahmarandhra*.

The Kundalini is dormant at the base of the spine, but when She is awakened, She moves upward through the *sushumnā nādī*, until She reaches the brahmarandhra at the top of the head. The importance of the brain has been realized by the scientists as well as the sages. When you arrive at the top of the head, you experience a state that is free from both pain and pleasure.

People usually say, "I would like to become free from pain, but why do I need to be free from pleasure?" Pain and pleasure go together: Pain becomes pleasure and pleasure becomes pain. When you become free from both of these, you experience a state that is higher than either — the state of supreme discrimination. Here, we are speaking of "discrimination" from the spiritual standpoint, not political discrimination or social discrimination. Supreme discrimination is the awareness that the Truth is inside.

The *Shiva Samhitā* says:

> The great Goddess is of the form of the Absolute.
> All letters, from *a* to *ksha*, arise from Her.
> She is of the form of sound.

It is for this reason that we chant so much. Chanting is a celebration for us. The Kundalini is "of the form of sound," and chanting awakens each cell in which Her power resides.

There was a monastery in which there was a lot of chanting, and all the monks were vigilant, alert, and enthusiastic about their work. In fact, they worked sixteen hours a day. But then a reformed monk became head of the monastery. He thought, "Why chant? In the old days they did not have anything else to do; that is why they chanted." So he reduced the period of chanting to half an hour a day.

Very soon all the monks became thoroughly lazy. Their hours of work were reduced from sixteen to seven, then to five, and finally to four. After a while they all lost their health and began to complain of various pains and illnesses.

The head monk realized something was wrong, but he didn't know what to do about it. Then he found out that a scientist had done research on chanting and had discovered that chanting is the best medicine for the body. He asked the scientist to come to the monastery. Chanting was re-introduced, and once again the monks began to chant for many hours. Their cells were reawakened, their bodies and minds began to heal, and they were able to work with greater enthusiasm. Their old contentment returned.

This research was done quite recently. I read about it in a clipping from the religion section of a North American newspaper. Although the sages have spoken of the power of chanting again and again over the centuries, until the scientists say it, we don't believe it.

A great saint, Mirabai, said:

O my dear ones, drink the nectar of the Name!
Give up bad company.
Keep the company of the good.

The company of the good is called *satsang*. It is the company of the Truth: not just good company on the outside, but on the inside, too. We can escape from the outer world, but not from the inner world of our thoughts, which goes with us no matter where we go.

Once there was a crow that no one liked. The other crows resented the way he sang, the way he ate — they just didn't like the way he was. So he told his elders that he wanted to go somewhere else where people would love him.

The elders said, "Listen. That won't change anything. No matter where you go, you'll always be a crow."

"No, no," he said. "Here, people do not appreciate me enough. They don't know my worth. I always feel terrible, and I'm sick of it."

He flew to Hawaii, but when he got there, he experienced the same thing — no one liked him. If you do not change inside, it does not matter how many changes you make on the outside, even paradise will not make you happy.

So Mirabai says keep good company inside and maintain a good inner state. For this good state, this good company, we must awaken our inner energy. Otherwise, when we hear or see something outside that upsets us, we bring it inside, and we live a miserable life. When we keep good company inside, we have supreme discrimination.

Mirabai also says we should allow all lust, anger, pride, greed, and infatuation to sink in the ocean of God's name. When you keep good company, both on the outside and on the inside, you are not carried away by all these emotions. You become the color of the Truth.

The Kundalini exists in the form of sound, and She is awakened by chanting. The *Shrī Vidyā Antar Yāga* describes Her in this way:

> Contemplate Kundalini,
> Who is supreme Consciousness,
> Who shines like a flash of lightning,
> Who is as fine as the fiber of a lotus stalk,
> Who has the brilliant light of countless suns,
> And who is a shaft of light as cool as hundreds
>   of nectarean moonbeams.

When this force is awakened inside, countless suns and moons are awakened. Last night when I talked about the white light, someone wanted to know if he should be visualizing it. It is not a matter of *visualizing* the white light; when the Kundalini is awakened, there *is* light, an inner explosion.

A man came to the Intensive in Oakland, and on the final afternoon of the Intensive, during *darshan,* he said, "I came here as a skeptic, and I am still a skeptic. But I have a problem. This morning during meditation my whole body exploded into millions of rays of light. It lasted during the whole hour of meditation. But you see, I don't want to believe in it." He was very sincere. I have often seen that skeptics are more sincere than believers; they *believe* in their skepticism. Believers are not *sure* about their beliefs.

You do not have to visualize the white light; when the inner force is awakened, there is an explosion inside. This force is "as fine as the fiber of a lotus stalk." The scriptures say it is subtler than the subtlest, finer than the finest. A dense mind cannot grasp it; only supreme discrimination, very fine viveka, can discern it.

We are so used to our daily habits of mind that if anything unfamiliar appears, we panic. In the modern age people call the inner force by this name or that name. They try to make it look "mystical" or exotic. But their jargon only belittles and waters down the reality of the mystical experience. This energy is very high: Because of Her outer aspect we can see and hear. She is the light behind the eyes, behind all the senses. Even though Her inner aspect is dormant in an ordinary person, all the senses derive their power from Her light. When the inner aspect is awakened, a miracle takes place; and, in one way or another, this miracle is talked about all the time, as people recognize the great changes that are taking place and try to come up with some reason for them.

Sound is one great way to awaken this energy. Turning within is also a great way. Receiving grace is the best way of all.

We spend most of our time thinking in a very trivial way:

"How are you doing?" we say.

"I am fine. How is your family?"

"Great."

"I had a toothache today, so I went to the dentist."

"My car ran out of oil. We got stuck on the highway and had to call the police."

"I ate so much pizza, I can hardly walk."

There is a beautiful story about the way we think. On the express train a young man stopped by Nasrudin's seat and asked, "Sir, can you tell me the time?"

Nasrudin looked at him and said, "Go to hell."

"What is the matter with you?" said the young man. "I ask you a civil question in a civil manner, and you give me such an outrageously rude answer. What's the idea?"

Nasrudin looked at him. He sighed and said, "Very well. Sit down. I will tell you. First, you ask me a question, so I have to give you an answer, right? Then you start a conversation with me about the weather, politics, and business. One thing leads to another. It turns out that we are both Jews. I live in the city; you are a stranger. Out of hospitality I ask you to my home for dinner. You meet my daughter, who is a beautiful girl — and you are a handsome man. You go out together a few times and fall in love. Finally, you come to ask for my daughter's hand in marriage. Now, why go to all that trouble? Let me tell you right now, young man: I will never let my daughter marry a man who doesn't even own a watch!"

This is our life. Someone comes along and says, "The Kundalini, this dynamic force, is inside you. When it is awakened, all the senses are purified, and great joy courses through the veins of your body. Everything becomes beautiful. Your speech changes. Your thinking becomes sublime. Your inner and outer worlds become one. Everything is perfect."

And you say, "Oh, really?"

It is so hard to believe, so hard to accept. For this reason, the sages and the scriptures say that you need yearning, you need longing for the experience. When you have this great yearning, everything happens spontaneously and naturally.

Last night I sang from a poem in which the seeker was praying to the Lord, "Give me one spark; that is all I need. If You give me just one spark, I know my life will change." In this same song, he also says:

> O Lord, You have given light to the sun
>   and to the moon.
> Why have You kept my little furnace in darkness?
> My furnace is so small;
> All that it needs is just one little spark.

This is yearning: wanting to see that light inside, wanting the inner experience, wanting to see God, wanting to feel the Truth. "Just one spark, O Lord, nothing more!" The seeker continues:

> O Lord, I am so cold!
> My whole body is shivering.
> I am losing my patience.
> I need one spark for a very small furnace.
> O Lord of fire, awaken my inner fire.

In all scriptures and philosophies you find this prayer: "Awaken my inner light, awaken my inner fire." This is the longing for the awakening of the energy inside.

We pray to the Lord for a miracle. We pray to the Virgin Mary for a miracle. We pray to the saints for a miracle. But have we ever thought of asking for the miracle of this inner awakening which will never leave us? The awakening of the light is the inner miracle; once we experience it, we live in a constant miracle, no matter where we are. What is not possible becomes possible. Our lives, inner and outer, become one.

After his experience of the inner awakening, the saint Allama Prabhu said, "Unimaginable, the light in the eye!" When you see the inner light, even the outer light becomes brighter. Everything shines with light.

Someone asked Baba, "Baba, what do you see when you look at me?"

Baba said, "I see the light in you."

The person said, "How can that be, Baba? I am an angry person. I am terrible. You must see all that."

Baba said, "No. I see light."

Light is more powerful than our emotions and feelings. When this light is awakened we understand our emotions and feelings. We are not made up of them at all; we are made of light. When this light is awakened with great force, then we see light everywhere.

Allama Prabhu also said, "Indescribable, the ringing in the ear!" When this energy is awakened you hear music, and that inner music is so beautiful.

In San Francisco, Baba visited a hospital for a checkup. There was a woman who had been in that hospital for many months because of a brain tumor. She had never before met an Indian Guru, or a swami — let alone Baba. When she saw Baba she began to feel a tingling sensation in her tumor.

She walked up to Baba and asked him, "Do you know me?"

Baba looked at her and said, "No."

She asked, "Then why are you doing this to me?"

When Baba asked her what was happening to her, she started crying. The person who was with Baba gave her a mantra card and told her, "Repeat this mantra."

She took it and kept repeating the mantra day after day, day after day. She started hearing the inner music, and she began to forget the pain. Her sorrow began to leave her. Her parents, who visited her all day long, couldn't understand what was happening. For the first few days, they thought she was probably going crazy. When you are happy, you are considered crazy; when you are unhappy, you are normal.

As the days passed, she stopped complaining about the pain, and the doctors said that she was getting better; the tumor had become smaller. Of course, then her parents became interested in Baba. When she came out of the hospital, they all went together to see him at the Oakland Ashram.

She said to Baba, "What music! How did you do that? Will I hear this music all the time?"

Baba said, "Yes."

She went home and the music grew louder and louder.

Two years later she telephoned Baba and said, "The music is getting louder and louder and I am feeling better and better. The doctors have told me that the little tumor I have in my brain will never leave me. Just as you have created this music inside me, now I ask you to finish my body in this music."

Baba told her, "Don't think about dying. Just keep listening to the music."

A month later she wrote a letter in which she said, "I know you are a great man. Just as you have created this music inside me, now you must give me another miracle."

Baba never answered the letter. A week later, her parents called and said, "She died while listening to the mantra." When she died, they saw light fill the whole room. It was an incredible thing, because at precisely the time when this happened to her, Baba had said, "She is merging. She is becoming one with the Absolute."

"Indescribable, the ringing in the ear!" There is so much power in the inner music. It has the power to give life and sustenance, and it also has the power of dissolution.

"Incomparable, the taste on the tongue!" When this inner power is awakened, everything you eat has a wonderful taste. In fact, you constantly taste sweetness in the throat. And this sweetness in the body does not come just from being sweet to people; it is a genuine experience throughout the entire being.

Allama Prabhu continues:

> When the Kundalini is awakened inside,
> You will find the Lord everywhere:
> In the tiniest particle of dust,
> In hard wood, or in a tender blade of grass.
> The Lord is everywhere:
> The subtle, the imperishable,
> The unchanging Principle.

The awakening of the energy is the greatest miracle. Then we live in supreme discrimination. This is the true miracle, because it frees us from both pain and pleasure. This is the highest state. There is no more boredom, no more loneliness. When people say that even though they meditate they still experience boredom, that means they are not meditating! And when people say they have received Shaktipat, yet they still feel lonely, that means there is still a long way to go.

Baba's mission is to allow everyone to experience the inner Truth. Shaivism says, "As above, so below. As outside, so inside." Therefore, we observe the discipline of chanting, of awakening the energy through the form of sound, and then merging into the sound.

We will chant the mantra *Om Namah Shivāya*. If you chant with your entire being, you will notice your body straightening up as you are chanting. The sound does the work: you do not even have to do it mentally. This has nothing to do with the power of suggestion.

When you chant the mantra, close your eyes and go very deep inside. Let the force in the mantra and the force within you become one.

Last night I said, "When we are sitting quietly in meditation, contemplate 'What am I?' " A newcomer came in the darshan line and said he had had the experience "I am that I am." It was his first time here. I said to him, "So, you have come here to enjoy the fruit of all our practices? We have been sitting here meditating for so many nights to have that experience!"

It is there, so try it. Chant the mantra *Om Namah Shivāya*, and in meditation feel every pore of the body. Do not think of the body as insignificant. There is light in every pore. Hear the sound in every cell. That will be our meditation for tonight.

Once again, with great respect and love, I welcome you all with all my heart.

Sadgurunāth Mahārāj kī Jay!

When You See
the Face of the Truth

Atlanta, March 22, 1986

WITH GREAT RESPECT AND LOVE, I welcome you all with all my heart. The mantras we chant at the beginning of the program are a prayer to the Lord in the Sanskrit language. The last verse says:

> Om. May we, Guru and disciple,
>   be protected together.
> May we be nourished together.
> May we achieve strength together.
> May our knowledge turn into light.
> May we never lose patience with one another.

When we pray to God in our own language, whether it is English, Spanish, or French, we often feel, "I cannot do it." However, when we pray in a language that we do not know, we feel that the Lord is listening and that something is really happening! This is the nature of the human mind. Whatever we know we take very lightly; whatever we do not know we feel has great importance.

As you get to know and experience Siddha Yoga, you realize it contains a very simple truth. In the beginning you might think that it is esoteric or beyond your reach, or that it is foreign and strange, but when the experience of the Self takes place, you realize how close it is to you. There is nothing foreign and nothing strange about that experience, because we are all one, and we are all that same Self.

One of the qualities we can have that will allow us to make greater progress on the spiritual path is persistence. When we keep trying and do not give up, the Lord has compassion on us and He bestows His grace. What gives us the strength to keep going? Swami Muktananda taught us that meditation gives us courage. He said, "Turn inside. There is so much strength, so much beauty, so much divinity, so much greatness inside." His message was: "Meditate on your own Self. Worship your own Self. Kneel to your own Self. Understand your own Self. Respect your own Self. God dwells within you as you."

This is an age-old message: God is within, beauty is within, divinity is within. However, just saying it is not enough. We have to contemplate it. It is said that man is what he thinks. Whatever you think about, whatever feeling you habitually entertain, you become that. When people want to imitate others, they contemplate them, thinking constantly about their activities and their movements until they begin to resemble the person. In the same way, when you contemplate the Truth, you become the Truth.

What is the Truth? We have heard so many truths in our lives: father speaks the truth, mother speaks the truth, sister speaks the truth, a child speaks the truth, and our teachers speak the truth. What is the Truth? Truth is that which never changes. It is as simple as that. Most of the truths that people talk about do change, so they cannot be the ultimate Truth. The ultimate Truth is within, and so we are told to turn inside. The ultimate Truth is always full, never empty. In the ultimate Truth there is no loneliness. It is always absolutely satisfying.

People used to come to Baba and ask him for blessings, saying, "Baba, I need a soul mate!"

Baba would ask, "What?"

We are always looking for companionship and friendship, and we feel our soul needs a mate. But the soul is full. It is so full it does not need a mate. It is the Friend, it is the Companion. For this reason, we turn within.

In the *Bhagavad Gītā*, Arjuna tells Lord Krishna that he is too afraid to fight. This happens to us also: We want to give up because we are afraid that if we find God we will lose our fame, our name, our friends. We are not afraid of losing God, of course, because we do not know Him. Lord Krishna tells Arjuna, "Go within. Then you will know your duty."

When you go within, you realize what it is that you really want to attain in life. If you do not reach this source within, you are attracted to something and then realize that you do not want it after all. You hear about something that you decide you must have, but as soon as you get it, you realize it is worthless. You move from one thing to another, realizing that no one thing is exactly what you want. For this predicament, you need inner guidance, you need inner strength.

The Lord said:

In this very world, everything is overcome
By those minds which rest in the Lord,
  in equality-consciousness.

The Absolute, the Lord, is untainted. The Absolute is pure. When we meditate on that which is pure, untainted, changeless, we get incredible strength from within.

An old lady was sitting on a chair, knitting away, when suddenly an earthquake struck, and she saw that a big piano was going to fall onto her little grandchild. She was quite an elderly lady, and she was not able to walk fast or even to speak quickly. But when she saw the piano about to fall and crush the child, she immediately got out of her chair and held up the piano so the child could escape. The child was saved, and the old lady let the piano fall. The earthquake continued. She walked very slowly back to her chair and sat down. When the tremors stopped, she went back to her knitting.

What happened? For one moment she had released an incredible power within herself. This kind of strength is available to us all the time but we do not consciously perceive it or try to develop it. Only when we are able to make it conscious can we apply it to every situation at every moment, can we experience it all the time.

For this reason we meditate on that which is pure and untainted; we meditate on the Truth. The Truth is called "grace," it is called "blessing," it is called "divine power." It has many names, but it is one Truth, it is one experience.

Lord Krishna tells Arjuna:

Meditate on this Truth.
Gaining strength from within,
You will have no fear.

Once a saint visited a king for a few days. When the time came to leave, he asked the king, "What would you like?" The saints always grant a boon to those who have offered them hospitality.

The king said to the saint, "You are such a renunciate. What do you have to give me? I already have everything. Here, take this stick from me instead. Give it to the first fool you come across."

The saint agreed. He took the stick and left, and although he traveled for twelve years from place to place, he could not find a fool. Finally one day, he drew near the palace again, and he heard that the king was about to die. He went to the king immediately and found him on his deathbed.

He said, "O King, I have been traveling for twelve years, but I haven't found a single fool in this world worthy of your stick. Here, you take it. You're the biggest fool I have come across."

The king asked, "What are you saying?"

The saint asked him, "Have you prepared for the next world?"

The king said, "No."

"There you are!" the saint said. "In this world you had everything you wanted, but what are you going to do after you die? Where are you going to go? You have never thought about it."

Contemplation of the Truth is for both this world and the next — for when we are alive and for when we leave our bodies. It is said over and over again that we cannot take anything external with us when we die; not even the tiniest possession goes with us — only what we have attained inside. Only the experience of God, the experience of the Truth, goes with us no matter where we go.

> Let a person uplift himself by his own Self;
> Let him not lower himself.
> The Self alone is one's friend,
> And the Self alone is one's enemy.

We think someone is our friend and someone else is our enemy. Nevertheless, the scriptures say, "You are your own friend. You are your own enemy." Whatever you grow inside becomes yours. If you sow the seed of love, you will reap love. If you sow the seed of hatred, you will reap hatred. This is one of the great teachings: We can become happy by being our own friend, and we can become very unhappy by being our own enemy. Outer friends can give us consolation and support. However, when we return to our room, we are alone. An outside enemy can give us trouble, can harass us, but when we go back to our room, there is no enemy. Again, we are alone. So if we are happy with ourselves, we are our own friend. If we are unhappy with ourselves, we become our own enemy.

Before coming here, we went to South Fallsburg. We had not told anyone we were coming, so we walked into an almost empty building.

However, the energy was pulsating, vibrating. That energy is awakened in a place after you have chanted and meditated there. In ancient times, they used to worship the land to awaken the energy. Then the place becomes your friend, and you feel supported and protected there.

In the same way, once you awaken the energy inside, whenever you close your eyes, you feel support and inspiration from within. Suddenly, you have all the ideas, you have all the plans, as if someone had laid them out for you. This is the power of meditation and contemplation. When you attain this, you become your own friend. You do not need to become your own enemy. Instead, become your own friend and experience incredible love.

> The Self is the friend of a person
> Who has conquered his senses;
> But for one who has not done so,
> The Self acts as an enemy.

When you conquer your senses and make them do what you want them to do, you experience the Truth, and you experience support and friendship. Otherwise, you feel that everything is going wrong. You want to go west, yet somehow you are going north. You want to go south; somehow you are going east. You experience an inner division, and you continually say, "I am of two minds."

Why are you not one-pointed? Because you have not experienced the strength of your own inner source, the grace of God, His blessing from within. You feel you are not what you should be. You do not feel what you should be feeling, because you are not gaining strength from the right source. You do not have the right motive, you do not have the right center.

In meditation you look for this center, the wellspring of the Truth, the wellspring of love; once you find it, you are a different person. When you see the face of the Truth, your life is transformed. People say that when you come in touch with the Guru, your life is transformed, but actually, it is when you see the face of the Truth within yourself that your life is transformed. That is a *real* transformation, and when you experience that, you never give up.

Two frogs, father and son, fell into a pail of milk one day. They were swimming around and around, until the father said, "I'm getting weaker. I can't go on."

The son said, "O father, don't give up. Something will happen."

The father said, "I can't." And he turned over and died.

The son had a young body and more enthusiasm. He kept swimming. In the meantime, the liquid became harder and harder. The pail was full of buttermilk, so the more he swam, the harder it became. Finally he stood on it and jumped out.

Going inside may be hard in the beginning, but if you keep trying, you are bound to find something, and this *something* will be the Truth. So turn inside. Discover the source. Find your own strength. We have glimpses of it every now and then. Make the experience of your own strength constant, so that you can get the best out of life.

The best is in everyone. We can have the best or the worst; however we choose to use our abilities, that is what we get. Seeing God in our own being is getting the best. Ruining this body is getting the worst. Seeing Consciousness, the power of God in this world, is getting the best. Seeing only misery is getting the worst. By continually going inside, we discover the best, the highest, the most sublime.

> With his mind harmonized by yoga, by reunion,
> The yogi sees the inner Self abiding in all beings,
> And all beings, in the Self.
> He sees the same One everywhere.

The scriptures teach not only the attainment of God, but also the purification of the mind. They continually say that if you purify your mind and have clarity of perception, you perceive God. Often our minds become restless, and we are not able to see things clearly. Things *are* clear, but our perception of them is not clear. The situation itself does not need to change, but our perception needs to change.

When we meditate, our intellect becomes sharper and our mind becomes sharper. As the intellect and the mind become clearer and sharper, we are able to perceive situations in a much better way. Yesterday I was speaking to someone who analyzes people's dreams. He said that after he met Baba Muktananda, his whole perception changed. He realized that we are made up of good and bad habits. At times we want to get rid of our bad habits; nevertheless, it is very difficult for us, because every habit has to be replaced by another. When he heard Baba say, "Repeat the mantra *Om Namah Shivāya,*" he realized that what Baba was doing was replacing our bad habits with the mantra.

A lot of people say, "I repeated the mantra a few times, and now I feel different. Amazing and miraculous things have been happening.

How does it work?" People used to ask Baba this question, and Baba would say, "It is just grace; it is God's blessing. Keep doing the mantra, and don't worry."

However, there is a scientific explanation for every occurrence. The mantra is purified energy. Each syllable of the mantra is made up of nothing but pure energy. When we repeat it, bad habits fall away automatically, and we are filled with that energy. When we replace our bad habits with pure energy, a different experience occurs, an incredible transformation takes place.

The Lord says:

There is nothing whatsoever
Higher than I am.
All this is strung on Me
Like clusters of gems on a string.

When we turn inside to meditate and contemplate, when we get in touch with our inner divinity, this is our experience of life: We are all gems on the necklace that is God. For this reason, at times we feel as if we have met one another before. There is this connection between us. Through meditation we become aware of it, and we experience again and again that we are jewels strung on the one string of the Truth.

Lord Krishna says:

I am the wetness in water,
I am the light in the moon and the sun,
I am the sound in all syllables and in ether,
And strength in all people;
I am the sweet fragrance of the earth,
The brilliance in fire, the life in all beings,
And the austerity in seekers.

This is what I like best: "the austerity in seekers." No matter how hard you find the practices, if you keep trying, you will find the Truth in your austerity. In effort there is attainment. In effort is the goal. Baba used to say, "The practice itself is the goal." Your work itself is the goal. It is not that you are working and working and one day you attain the goal. Your work, your duty, *is* the goal. When you turn inside, this becomes completely clear.

Baba liked to tell a story about a woman who lost her necklace: A woman was cooking one day when a wedding procession went by.

There was a big band, and a lot of singing and dancing. Very excited, she went outside to see what was happening. She watched the whole thing, and then she went back indoors. Suddenly she realized she had lost her necklace. She looked for it everywhere. She went from one room to another, but she could not find it.

She began to scream and shout, "I've lost my necklace! I've lost my necklace!"

Her friends and neighbors hurried into her house and asked, "What's happening?"

She said, "I've lost my necklace! I've lost my necklace!"

One of her friends said, "That's too bad."

"I know! I know!" she said. "What will I tell my husband? I lost my necklace! I lost my necklace!"

In the meantime, another friend saw something shiny around her neck and asked, "What's this?"

She said, "Oh! It's my necklace!"

The writer says that the necklace had never been lost — there was only a big commotion. In the same way, we have never lost the grace or love of God. We just like to make a big fuss: "I'm so lonely. I'm so miserable. I'm so poor. Nobody loves me!" There is so much strength, so much love, so much grace inside.

A poet says that if you think you cannot find love, if you do not discover grace immediately, then follow this path:

> When you speak, weigh your words;
> Then you earn the right fruit.
> When you walk, make sure
> You are taking the right steps
> And that your head is not held too high.
> This world is choked with thorns,
> But it is also full of flowers.
> Fill your basket with flowers, with love.
> As for the thorns — burn them
> And fill your basket with flowers.
>
> When you speak, weigh your words;
> Then you earn the right fruit.
> This world is full of rocks,
> And some of them are shiny.

The rocks that you see are ordinary,
But there are jewels, too.
Collect those jewels;
Let go of the rocks.

When you speak, weigh your words;
Then you earn the right fruit.
See your own Self in this entire universe.
Don't get stuck in analyzing
What is good and what is bad,
Don't get trapped in that duality.
Understand that you are in this world
And that the world is within you.
When you have this understanding,
You won't live in your ego.

When you speak, weigh your words;
Then you earn the right fruit.
Welcome everyone with great love
And with great respect.
Have this feeling of oneness toward
Everyone and everything.
Don't keep God outside you.
Let God be your own breath,
The breath that you inhale and exhale.
If you have this understanding,
Then you have attained the Truth.

I see that people have done a lot of work here at the Center. They
have awakened even the pillars in this room with color. When we give
color to life, there is joy and love. A lot of work and a lot of time must
have gone into the decorations. If you also give yourself the time to go
inside, you will see incredible colors within. When we turn within and
experience that the Consciousness within us is also within everyone
else, we do not have to fight. Not everyone can understand it right
away, but at least one of us at a time can understand it, then another,
and then another. In this way, eventually there will be many, and then
this experience will not be just inside, but outside, too.

We will chant the mantra *Om Namah Shivāya* to replace our old habits. Then we will sit quietly for five minutes. As we sit quietly, try to experience the inner pulsation. It is very subtle. When you close your eyes you might feel that you are seeing darkness, and that there is nothing else. It is all right. Just sit in that stillness. In that stillness there is light. In that stillness there is love. In that stillness there is the greatest attainment.

Once again, with great respect and with great love, I welcome you all with all my heart.

Sadgurunāth Mahārāj kī Jay!

A Clean Heart
Reflects the Light of God

Atlanta, March 24, 1986

WITH GREAT RESPECT AND LOVE, I welcome you all with all my heart. Again and again, you have heard the words *Sadgurunāth Mahārāj kī Jay!* "I hail the Master who has revealed the Truth to me." Why do we keep saying this? As human beings, we have a tendency to be quite ungrateful — ungrateful to our parents, to our children, to our school, to our society. No matter how much our parents offer us, no matter how much the school gives us, our ingratitude persists. Because we are ungrateful, we are not able to experience happiness, we are not able to experience love or serenity. We are always thinking, "They never gave me enough." But on the spiritual path, since whatever we receive, great or small, is always the Truth, we say, "I hail the Master who has revealed the Truth to me."

When we become grateful, we receive more. When we show our gratitude, we receive even more. This is the law of nature. On the other hand, as we become more and more unthankful, we receive less and less. It is good to question, but when we go so far as to deny what we have received, we also lose it. This is why we continually say, "I hail the Master. I hail the Lord." And having this fountain of gratitude, we receive more and more. It is as simple as that.

We have come here to meditate and to chant. Although we are listening to a talk, our main purpose is to turn within and find our own divinity. No matter how much divinity we see in others, if we do not see the divinity within ourselves, it is useless. In Nature there are magnificent waterfalls and rivers, exquisite plants, delightful animals and birds. Nevertheless, if we cannot experience joy inside, no matter how much beauty there is outside, we cannot enjoy it.

This is why we meditate: We turn within to realize that the same beauty that has manifested outside us manifests within us also. Only when we have this beautiful experience inside can we really experience the beauty outside.

What prevents us from seeing the beauty within and without? Everything we have collected for years on end, lifetime after lifetime. A great saint, Tulsidas, gives a list. He says we have accumulated desires, which prevent us from experiencing the Truth, from seeing God. We have accumulated pride, which prevents us from experiencing the inner vision. Our pride says, "I am just a mediocre human being. How can God dwell within me?" Or, "There is so much suffering. How can God exist in this pain?" Tulsidas says that the pride we have accumulated becomes a veil of delusion which keeps us from seeing the Truth. We have also accumulated greed, aversion, hatred, deception, and pretension. When we have collected all this, how can we see God? How can we experience love for one another? Whatever faults we have within ourselves we project upon others. For this reason, just as we cannot recognize that God exists within us, we cannot believe that He exists within anyone else.

One of our accumulated qualities is deception. Baba told a beautiful story about a saint who used to say, "The deceiver falls for his own deception."

A rich man who heard this disagreed. One day he asked the saint, "What do you mean by saying 'You will fall for your own deception'? If you create deception, it is so that someone else will fall for it."

The saint said, "Why don't you put my words to the test?"

The rich man said, "Very well." He was very proud, very arrogant. He invited the saint to his house to eat, and he poisoned the food. This was his deception. But just before the saint arrived, the rich man's son came in and ate the food that his father had prepared. By the time the saint came, there was a dead body in the chair.

The saint looked at the rich man and said, "If there is deception, the deceiver falls for it."

This is exactly what happens. We think we are going to use the vices we have accumulated on someone else, but we ourselves fall prey to our vices. The truth is that the heart is a wish-fulfilling tree: whatever we think beneath it comes true.

Once a man who was very hungry and tired sat under a wish-fulfilling tree. After a while he thought, "How I wish I had some company. I'm so lonely." Right away, a beautiful woman appeared. Then he thought, "How I wish there were a house." Immediately, a house appeared. They went inside. "How I wish we had food to eat." Immediately a cook brought food, and they sat at the table.

When Baba told this story, he used to say that they could have just gone ahead and eaten their food. However, as the man picked up a morsel, he said, "My goodness! Everything I've thought has come true. There must be a devil here!" Immediately, a huge monster appeared. Naturally, the man was terrified and he screamed, "He's going to eat me up!" And so he did. Finished!

Living in this body is like being under a wish-fulfilling tree. The house of God is not far away. It is very close. Whatever we wish does come true. But if we make wishes while under the influence of all our accumulated habits of mind, then what we get is desire, pride, delusion, aversion, hatred, greed, deception, and pretension.

Tulsidas says God can be experienced in a heart which is free from all these habits. To become free from them we continually repeat God's name, chant, and perform service.

In the *Bhagavad Gītā*, Lord Krishna describes this as our duty, or *dharma*. If you are a monk, your dharma is to fulfill the duties of a monk. If you are a householder, your duty is to fulfill the dharma of family life. If you are working, that is your duty. But whatever your outer role may be, the true duty of each human being is to recognize the Truth in his or her own heart, and in turn to experience the same Truth in others.

This experience of God arises in a heart that is free from the accumulated traces of many lifetimes. You cannot have these destructive qualities and also constantly experience the Truth. You cannot be pure and deceptive at the same time. You cannot be experiencing the Truth while suffering. They are two different states. When you are experiencing the Truth, all suffering dissolves.

There was a king who wanted to know God, to see the Truth, but he couldn't give up the pride of his power and wealth. Nevertheless, he was a seeker. If you have yearning such as he had, then you have a dream or a vision, or an incident takes place which changes your whole life. One day when the king was asleep on the seventh floor of his palace, he heard a noise on the terrace outside his room. He went to see who it was, and he saw his Master. He asked, "What are you doing on my terrace?"

The Master said, "I am looking for my horse."

The king was puzzled. He asked, "Why are you looking for your horse on the terrace? Look for the horse where you lost it, not here on the seventh floor of the palace."

The Master said, "How can you be looking for God when you are a slave of sense pleasures, when you are living the high life?"

This sounds like a very simple question, but because of it the king recognized the Truth. Attaining the Truth is not just having a vision of light. It is perceiving the Truth in any situation.

Immediately, the king realized that he had to drop all of his accumulated possessions, and only then, in the clarity of his heart, could he experience the Truth.

Tulsidas tells us:

> You experience God in a heart
> Which wishes well for others.

The scriptures say, "O my mind, think well of yourself, and also think well of others." It is very difficult for human beings to wish others well, but this well-wishing is a very beautiful practice. We attribute it mostly to grandfathers and grandmothers. They say, "God bless you. Best wishes!" I remember an elderly person once came to me and said, "God bless you!" When you hear this it is so innocent, so simple and beautiful. Often elderly people come with such big smiles. Somehow it seems they have crossed the threshold of pettiness: they have experienced life, they have gone through all its troubles and its suffering, and so they want to wish others well. For this reason elderly people generally do experience God — at least to a certain extent. When you are very young, when you are hot-blooded, you feel that God, or divine love, is not for you. All your accumulated habits are for you. They are *your* possessions.

Only a heart which constantly wishes well can experience the Truth continuously. We receive so much from the people around us, from our Masters, from great beings, from the scriptures. Nevertheless, we are so fraught with desires and greed that we only throw mud on these beings and on the scriptures.

A well-known leader was traveling in a horse carriage when he came to a place where a great being was lying in the road. The leader got out of the carriage and went up to the saint. "How can you obstruct my carriage?" he said. "Move!"

The saint replied, "If I move, something unpleasant will be revealed. It would be better if you just took another road."

The leader was extremely arrogant. He said, "Don't you know who I am? You must obey my command."

The saint said, "All right," and he moved, taking with him his blanket, which had been covering all the heads that had been cut off by the leader.

The great beings give us a lot of protection. While we commit sins and make mistakes, their grace continues to protect us and allow us to survive. But our pride is such that we force them to reveal what we have done, rather than asking for grace or for blessings to overcome our shortcomings.

In order to wish others well, we have to have a heart that is free from all the possessions we have stored, because these possessions keep us tied to our actions and their consequences. Through our spiritual practices, we become free.

The awakening of the energy within is the awakening of the grace within. For this reason, when we go to a saint who has become free, we automatically receive a miracle, whether it is the healing of the body or of the mind. A clean heart continually reveals the light of God. Otherwise, we stay tied to past impressions.

A man wanted to cross a river by boat. The boat was very heavily laden, and when he tried to row it, it would not move. Not able to understand why, he emptied the boat completely. Still it would not move. He called some magicians. They repeated some syllables, but the boat would not move. He called some astrologers and asked for the auspicious time to move the boat. He waited for the correct moment, but the boat would not budge. He called some devotees to come and chant. Still the boat would not move. Finally, he called across to a certain man on the other shore. He recognized that this man was superior to other human beings. He never talked to anyone, but kept to himself. He just sat on the bank of the river minding his own business. The boatman asked this man, "Do you know why my boat does not move?"

"O boatman!" he replied, "Don't you see that the boat is still tied to the dock?"

It is the same with us. The Truth is so simple and so straightforward. We are always wondering, "Why don't I experience the love of Jesus? Why don't I experience the love of Krishna? Why don't I experience the love of my own inner Self?" Love is there, grace is there, but we are tied to our thoughts, concepts, feelings, and accumulated possessions.

We need a clean heart, which can reflect the Truth, which can reflect love, not just a few times each day or at night, but all the time.

The *Shiva Sūtras* say: *kathā japaha*, "Whatever a great being says is repetition of the mantra." When you have a clean heart, you speak nothing but the Truth. Whatever you say carries a message; it is nothing but light. When you have a clean heart, you experience the Truth when you are asleep and when you are awake; you experience the Truth in all your actions.

This is the reason Baba always said that to know God you don't have to give up your house or your daily work or your family. Of course, when you see some of us in orange robes, living the life of monks, you ask, "Why don't you practice what you preach?" The fact is that everyone has a different destiny. This world is nothing but a great stage, and every one of us plays a different role and has a different duty. To know God, we don't need to give up our role in the world. We only need to let go of the unnecessary possessions we have collected inside.

People get very scared. They say, "If I give up my ego, I will lose all my ambition. Then how can I work in this world?" It is not your ego, but your inner strength and energy that enable you to work. The ego does not cultivate the energy within. In fact, it reduces its strength. That is why Kabir says:

> Remove the veil of your ego,
> And then you will find your Beloved.

This is so true. When two people meet each other, if there is no veil, they immediately fall in love. However, two minutes later, the veil falls once again and they say, "I never loved you. I always knew it. You were the wrong person for me." Exactly the same thing happens when it comes to loving God. When we let go of the veil, we can easily love God; we can easily experience Him in everyone and everything.

Through meditation, through the power of turning inside, we practice self-inquiry: Why am I the way I am? Why do I do the things I do? As we ask these questions of ourselves, the God in the heart listens to our prayers. He hears our questions. And the answer always comes in the form of an experience. This experience removes our shortcomings and dissolves our veil. It frees us to communicate with one another and to love one another.

A saint said, "O Lord, there is nothing for me without Your grace." This is the quality of surrender, the quality of offering. But we cannot say this unless we become absolutely free, absolutely independent of all the things we have collected inside. This feeling, "O Lord, Your grace is everything, Your blessing is everything," does not come to us easily.

We all want to be self-made people. "I am a self-made man," a great writer said. "However, if I had to do it again, I would ask someone for help!" Only when we have become free inside can we pray to God, saying, "Your grace is everything for me," not just with our physical tongue, but with the voice of the heart.

Although turning within is a very simple act, it is the most difficult task of all. How many of you can just close your eyes and then say, "I went inside"? Try it. Close your eyes. Where does your awareness go? This is something you can start to discover. Some people close their eyes and fear the darkness within; others' minds race. Some people immediately get in touch with their emotions and feel like crying or laughing; still others experience nothing whatsoever. The act of closing the eyelids is the same, yet for each person the experience is different.

When we close our eyes, we give ourselves some time. The reason we are not in touch with the inner Self is that we are constantly running — running to impress the world, our colleagues, our partners. We are continually doing something to influence others, and as we do this, we forget who we are. We might think we are a man or a woman, but at a deeper level within there is no recognition of who we are. When we close our eyes and give ourselves some time, then the power of meditation, the awakened energy inside, works on whatever manifests — whether it is fear that arises, or thoughts and emotions, or nothing at all. Some people think that meditation is about suppressing our feelings and our thoughts. However, meditation frees us. It liberates us from whatever limits us.

Transformation does not always happen instantly, but as we pursue our practices daily, something really does happen: we become free from our anger and from our petty desires. It is crucial to permanently overcome whatever binds us. Otherwise, we may experience our greatness when we sit for meditation, but not during our daily lives. We have habits and impressions that have been accumulated over so many years and lifetimes. This is why sometimes even a very sweet person will say, "I don't know why I got angry. I never knew such a thing existed within me." Therefore, we constantly repeat the mantra.

As we go within, we face whatever exists within ourselves, and as we face it, we are able to overcome it. As we overcome it, we begin to experience lightheartedness. We become like little children, always happy. We grown-ups might experience an impending doom hanging over the world, but for little children life is play. They are absolutely free, and their voices and actions reflect only happiness.

Once a little boy pointed to my *bindi* and said, "Gurumayi, what's that dot on your forehead?" I didn't reply. He said, "Is it red color?" I nodded my head. Then he asked, "Were you drawing on your face, Gurumayi?" So I said, "Yes, I didn't have much to do today."

There is such freedom in children. There was nothing implied, nothing behind his words. It is different with adults; with them you always have to read between the lines. But with children, there is such freedom, such liberation, that nothing they say or do is binding. We need this kind of absolute, complete freedom that enables us to experience the Truth all the time, to live happily in this world, and to look our neighbors and colleagues in the eye.

Even though meditation is only a matter of closing your eyes and going inside, it is an act of purification. As we face ourselves inside, this purification takes place. Pilgrims bathe in holy rivers to become free from their impurities, but we do not become pure just by bathing the outer skin. It is necessary to become pure from within as well. When we have a clean heart, the love of God is constantly reflected in it. His light shines within us all the time.

Tulsidas, the great saint, says, "Once your heart is very clean, every breath, every inhalation and exhalation, is also the sound of God." We live in the sound of God. This is why the Bible says, "In the beginning was the Word." Through sound, the world came into existence; through sound, it is maintained; and finally, the world dissolves into sound. Similarly, we are created through the Word, maintained by it, and finally we merge back into it. This Word is not just a syllable. It is the essence of sound itself. By chanting we awaken every particle in the body. A sweet sound creates sweet vibrations. A harsh sound creates bitter vibrations. So when we chant the sweet sound of the name of God, it replaces all our negativities, all our accumulated impressions.

We will chant *Jay Jay Vitthal, Jaya Hari Vitthal.* "Hail to the Lord. Hail to the Lord." A lot of people ask me if they can repeat these chants in their own language. In North America they want to chant in English; in Mexico, in Spanish; in France, in French.

It is very natural to want to repeat these chants in the language with which you are familiar. For this reason, it is important to understand right from the beginning that it is not the language that matters, it is the sound. These syllables have been put together in order to create the right vibrations to awaken the inner energy. Nonetheless, the meaning of the words is also significant.

The word *Hari* means "the Lord who takes away the fluctuations of the mind." *Vitthal* means "the Lord who is firmly established within me." As we repeat these sounds again and again, we replace our bad habits with this sublime truth.

Jñāna yogis like to have only intellectual knowledge, whereas *bhaktas* prefer the heart's feelings of devotion. There are a lot of paths. However, Siddha Yoga encompasses all yogas. Through self-inquiry we follow the yoga of knowledge. We ask: Who am I? What am I doing? By constantly offering our love to God, to the world, and to other people, we are practicing *bhakti yoga*. And as we mentally repeat certain syllables again and again, we practice *mantra yoga*, the yoga of the Word.

If you cannot chant, just sit and listen. It is the sound vibration more than the words that makes the difference. A vibration can elevate you or bring about your downfall. Many times it is not what our friends say that matters to us, but what they are. The vibration is more important than the words.

As we chant, we purify our bodies as well as our minds. As the inner and outer purification takes place, it is easy for the light of God to shine. Then, even though we have a dense body, we can be transparent; even though we exist in one place, we are not stuck there.

With great respect, and with great love, I welcome you all with all my heart.

Sadgurunāth Mahārāj kī Jay!

O Lord, What Is This World?

Atlanta, March 26, 1986

WITH GREAT RESPECT AND LOVE, I welcome you all with all my heart. Night after night, you have heard these phrases. You have heard it all before, and so you block your mind to this welcome and spare yourself from listening. It is with *great* respect and with *great* love that you are welcomed, with *all* my heart. The reason you block it out of your mind is that you can't believe that someone is welcoming *you*. You can't believe that someone really loves you. You cannot accept the fact that someone you have never met *really* extends welcome in every sense of the word.

Once you block your mind toward one thing, you block it toward everything. Then, whether we are talking about God, about the inner Self, about love, or about the highest experience, you are constantly distracted, thinking of something else.

While praying to the Lord, the saint Bhartrihari asks: "What is this world? Is it poison or is it nectar?"

> I walk down the road:
> On one side I see beautiful people
>   talking to one another.
> On the other side I see people
>   fighting with one another.
> I walk down the road:
> On one side scholars are discussing
>   the Absolute.
> On the other side people are arguing
>   with each other over their daily lives.

I walk down the road:
People are singing to their hearts' content.
I look to the other side,
And people are totally dissatisfied —
All they want to do is kill themselves.
I walk down the road:
Babies are being born.
I look to the other side:
Old people are walking with canes.

O Lord, what is this world?
Is it poison or is it nectar?
How should I regard the world
    in which I live?
Duality, diversity, disharmony exist everywhere.
Where can I find peace?
What is the nature of this world?

The same thing happens here. Evening after evening we have talks, chanting, and meditation. On one side people have great experiences. On the other side people are totally confused. On one side people are chanting to their hearts' content. On the other side people are arguing. On one side people are ecstatic, absolutely delighted, experiencing the freedom of a lifetime. On the other side people are bound, totally entangled in their ideas of themselves.

What is life? Is it poisonous or is it nectarean? There is so much greatness, so much divinity! And on the other hand, there is so much petty behavior. Why is it that we prefer what is worse rather than what is better? What is it in the human mentality that does not allow us to experience the love of God, the love of the inner Self, the incredible treasure which lies within each person?

In the *Yoga Vāsishtha*, the sage says our suffering is caused by the unsteady mind.

This worldly life is not conducive to true happiness,
So reach the state of equanimity
In which you will experience peace, bliss, and truth.
If you stay within the unsteady mind,
Then there is no peace, there is no happiness.

We are always trying to find the truth, to "get at the facts." We feel, "If I know the facts, I'll know everything." And then we find out some of those facts and we feel, "I wish I didn't know that!"

The unsteady mind is always restless. It moves up and down, here and there, but it cannot find peace in this changing world where nothing and no one ever stays the same. A monk becomes a householder and a householder, a monk. A rich person becomes poor, a poor person, rich. A happy person grows unhappy, and finally becomes totally dejected.

Since this world is constantly changing, if you try to find lasting peace and ultimate joy in it, you cannot. This is why Baba kept saying, "Turn within. Meditate on your own Self." As we constantly hear this message, we become numb to it. We forget that the being who is teaching us has experienced all that he teaches. Having himself suffered through life, he tells us that joy, God, and the Truth all lie within, and that this Truth does not change. Yet somehow we totally ignore what he says.

Once someone asked Nasrudin, "How old are you?"

He said, "I'm forty."

The person said, "Nasrudin, you told me the same thing five years ago."

Nasrudin said, "I never change my word." The unchanging Truth is not like Nasrudin's truth. It is not just a matter of words. It must be experienced.

Turn within. Meditate on the Truth inside. It is only when you separate yourself from your habitual reality that you experience something higher, something more sublime, and are able to live in divinity. Then you no longer seek divinity — you *live in* divinity.

Baba had plenty of suffering. He performed his austerities. Sometimes he lived in a dilapidated house, sometimes in a comfortable house. Sometimes he was surrounded by impoverished people and sometimes by rich people. He kept the company of some who were intelligent and of others who were stupid. But he never changed his message. He traveled all over and always said, "Turn inside. Meditate on your own Self, which is the source of great joy."

A lot of us change in accordance with the company we keep. If we are with intelligent people, we start feeling, "I am very intelligent because all my friends are intelligent." If we are with stupid people, we feel, "I must be an idiot because everyone around me is stupid."

But a being who has realized the Truth never changes his message according to situations or people. Baba continually said one thing: "Turn within."

The mind is unsteady. If you look for facts, for truths in this changing world, your suffering will only increase. But as you separate yourself from outer phenomena and find the unchanging Truth, you are able to live in the changing world.

Kabir sang:

Where do you look for Me?
O My dear one, I am always with you.
I am so close to you. I am with you.

Once we find that Truth inside, we can recognize the same divinity, the same beauty outside us. We can see this world as the play of God. And we can understand why there is duality.

A lotus is so beautiful, yet it grows in a muddy pond. A rose is so beautiful, but surrounding it are thorns. In the same way, the temple of God lies within the body. Once we recognize the divinity inside ourselves, we can also see the same Truth outside in the world. We can understand the paradox that the God who is beyond duality exists in the world of duality as well.

A great saint, Ram Tirth, put it this way:

Pass through the crowded streets and cities in the same way you pass through beautiful landscapes and lovely mountains. Enjoy everything, despite all the criticisms and jealousies of others, which are like slippery ground and falling rocks. Be unaffected, a witness.

How can you be unaffected by this world? It is only possible if you have experienced your own divinity. If you look at the lives of all the saints and great beings, there was turmoil and conflict around them. Even Socrates, who was a great scholar, had a wife who constantly got angry with him.

One day a friend said to him, "Socrates, you are such a great man, so learned. Why do you stay with this woman? She is ruining your life!"

Socrates said, "No. She is my greatest teacher. I must have her around to keep me down to earth."

The friend said, "I don't see how you can live with her."

At that moment, Socrates' wife stormed into the living room and yelled at him for not washing the dishes. He listened and listened but he didn't budge. Then she brought buckets of water and began dumping them on him.

Socrates looked at his friend and said, "What a marvelous creature! Don't you see? She defies the laws of nature. She thunders and rains at the same time!"

The only reason he could perceive divinity in such an action is that he recognized something greater in his wife. When you experience divinity, you can remain unaffected by outer disturbances.

We feel that this world is a tragedy. Everywhere we turn, nothing seems to be working right. Everything is falling apart. But we perceive the world as tragic only because of the preoccupations of our wavering minds. Not only is one's own mind unsteady, but so is everyone else's. You have one concept and everyone else has a different concept. Even partners cannot agree. No wonder the world seems chaotic.

We need to experience God's divinity in our own hearts, not just when we pray but all the time, not just when we have committed sins but every second of our lives. When we stay in touch with this beauty, with this divinity, we can live in laughter and love, and we can share this Truth with everyone. The mind is unsteady, but the experience of God is constant.

The sage Vasishtha says:

> Liberation brings the coolness of peace,
> Whereas bondage is a fire that scorches the mind.
> Even after realizing this, people do not strive for liberation.
> How foolish they are!

When he says "Liberation brings the coolness of peace," Vasishtha is describing not just another concept, but a continuing experience.

One evening a man came in the *darshan* line and gave me a letter. When I went home, I read the letter in which he cursed God because his wife was in the hospital dying of cancer. He said he did not want to lose her, but since he knew she was going to die, he felt there was no such thing as a God of mercy. He began to rationalize his disbelief in God: "A child wants to look up to someone," he wrote, "and the child thinks his parents are perfect and makes them his deities. As he grows up, he is always searching for some hidden, higher power to replace them, until he says, 'The unseen force is God.' So God is just an idea. Everyone wants something superior, so we ourselves create something unseen and unknown — the idea of God."

I was very interested in this letter, and I also realized the person who wrote it was in a terrible predicament. I wished that he would come back, and he did. The second time he met me I said, "I read your letter, but I don't agree with you," and he said to me, "Well, I don't agree with you either." Then he said, "Listen, Gurumayi, I just want to keep my wife. I love her. She is beautiful. She has given me everything, and I don't want to lose her, even for God."

I said to him, "Why don't you just keep coming?" I gave him a rose and said, "Take this to your wife." And he did.

We didn't agree with each other, but he kept coming night after night, and he kept chanting and sitting for meditation. And as the nights rolled by, he began to drop his negativity.

What was happening was that although his wife was dying of cancer, as she started seeing a change in him — a change he didn't even notice in himself — she became happier and happier. She told him how happy she was for him, though she had to leave this world. And their relationship began to improve, it began to go through an incredible change. The man kept on coming for the whole three months I was in his area. Finally one night she died. And though this happened, he didn't die; before her death, his awareness had shifted within.

He came and told me, "Gurumayi, I believe that God does exist." With tears in his eyes he said, "My wife gave me the experience that God truly exists." Later, he came and saw me in another city, and he was a changed man, absolutely changed.

The miracle was unseen, unknown. Although the man did not suddenly forget his *concept* — that God is only a name for an unseen force we cannot understand — his *experience* was solid, absolutely concrete: liberation. Through meditation a person is freed from his fixed ideas.

It isn't that God is an idea; it is that you have the *idea* that God is an idea. As you liberate yourself from that idea, you experience peace. The man liberated himself from the idea that the God in whom he didn't believe was taking his wife away from him. When he separated himself from this concept, he experienced peace. Later on he was able to give that peace and love to his children, and they were able to cope with her death, with separation, because their father had experienced an internal separation from his own fixed ideas. Because of this inner separation, he experienced union with God, union with divinity.

The experience of God might not be a visible miracle, a known miracle. It is an unseen, unknown miracle that creates this experience. We arrive at the experience of God as we free ourselves from what we think we are and are not, what we think the world is and is not. Then we recognize the God within ourselves and the God within others. Only then can we love one another freely. Otherwise our love is conditional: "I will love you if you will love me in this way. I can give you this much if you give this much to me." Conditions, conditions, conditions. We live within these conditions. We have to become free, we have to be liberated from these limitations.

On another occasion a woman came in the darshan line and asked me, "Gurumayi, are you a liberated woman?"

I realized that there was a double meaning to her words. That night I hadn't spoken about liberation, so the question didn't arise from my talk. She kept standing there. People kept coming and moving away, and she just stood there looking at me. I wouldn't give her an answer. Then she took her bag and put it over her shoulder and said, "I guess I will have to find out on my own." I was so relieved, because the scriptures say that if you say, "I'm liberated," you are not. If you are liberated, then who is saying you are liberated? For this reason they say, *nihshabdam brahma*, "The Absolute is free from all words and all sounds." You can't say this about it, and you can't say that. *Neti neti*, "not this, not that." You can't say "I'm liberated," and you can't say, "I'm not liberated." If you say, "I'm liberated," there is still bondage; and if you say, "I'm not liberated," how can there be bondage, because you have the understanding that you are not liberated. So we go for the experience, not the words which are neither this nor that.

When there is absolute liberation, there is incredible peace, incredible serenity. Then you can be fully alive even in times of calamity. Otherwise, you can be dead even when there is no conflict.

The sage Vasishtha continues:

He who is able to battle successfully
Against a mighty army is not a hero.
Only he who is able to cross the ocean
Known as the mind and senses is a hero.

If you just win a battle fighting soldiers, you are not a true hero. If you are a slave to your senses and to your mind, how can you be a hero? It is possible to give great talks and have great, entertaining conversations with people, but then, when you go home and you are by yourself, you experience loneliness and depression. This is why we need stability, serenity. We can use great words and beautiful gestures, we can use brilliant tactics and strategies, we can win people over, and we can satisfy them — but what about ourselves? Who is going to satisfy us, our own mind, our own senses? It is for this reason the sage Brahmananda says:

> Wake up! At least now, wake up!
> Wake up to your own Self,
> Awaken to your own reality.

There is love and divinity within you, but it isn't enough that they should remain in the cave of the heart. They must course through your veins and your blood cells and permeate your entire being so that you can experience joy at all times, when you are alone as well as when you are with people. To experience this independent joy, pursue your practices, day in and day out. The experience has to permeate not just our minds but our entire being. Great words are not enough; the experience has to remain when we are silent also.

That experience is within you. Don't doubt it. The *Yoga Vāsishtha* says:

> As long as there are sesame seeds,
>   there is oil.
> As long as the body exists,
>   the different moods will also exist.
> If a person rebels against the states
>   that the body is naturally subject to,
> It is like trying to cut space to pieces
>   with a sword.

The body undergoes many changes, and so does the mind. The world is constantly changing too, and in this changing world we have to find peace. A lot of people feel, "Once the world is harmonious and at peace, I'll find peace and harmony within myself, in my personal life, and in my family life." Many people have been waiting for so many years, waiting for peace in the outer world so that they can experience it within.

A great saint used to pray to the Lord, "O Lord, give me the energy to change this world." Later he said: "Many years passed by and I was middle-aged. I realized I no longer had enough strength to change the

116

world. I was no longer young and rebellious. So I began to pray to the Lord, 'O Lord, give me enough energy to change my relatives.' I became an elderly person, and I realized I didn't even have enough strength to change my relatives. They were much younger and much stronger than I. So then I began to pray to the Lord, 'O Lord, give me enough strength so that I can change myself.' Only then was I satisfied. So, I warn you, pray to the Lord right in the beginning: 'O Lord, give me the energy to change myself.' "

If we can change ourselves, then everything else will follow. If we are waiting for peace and harmony in the world, we'll be waiting for many, many centuries. If we start with ourselves, we can experience peace and harmony immediately. Just as there is fire in wood, there is peace within this body. The Self, God, is within this body.

Vasishtha continues:

> Consciousness minus conceptualization
>   is the eternal Absolute.
> Consciousness plus conceptualization
>   is thought.

As long as you attach an idea to Consciousness, it is an idea; it's just a thought. If you separate Consciousness from your thought, then it is the Absolute. But once you are established in that experience, then you will be able to see God in every thought, in every feeling, and in every person. It is not to keep ourselves away from ourselves that we separate Consciousness from thought; but this separation is necessary in the beginning so that we can experience divinity. Once we experience divinity, this separation is no longer necessary. Then we can stay with our thoughts and experience the Truth at all times.

The *Vijñāna Bhairava* gives a beautiful centering technique. It says that if you follow this technique, you will be able to conquer your senses:

> The seeker should free his mind of all support
> And refrain from all thought.

Free your mind from everything, even from the idea that you have the floor to sit on. Do it now. Totally free your mind from everything that makes you believe that you exist. Then the state of pure Consciousness will arise. Pure Consciousness is the support of all. Consciousness itself is without support, without attachment, without definition. Any idea you have of being a man or a woman, any feeling which makes you believe you are happy or unhappy, any thought which makes you feel that you exist or do not exist — for a moment, let go of these things.

Totally separate yourself from your mind, even if it is racing. In practicing this separation, there is liberation, and in this liberation there is union.

Once, when I was staying by the ocean, I saw people flying through the air with the help of parachutes. As they floated down to touch the sand, there was an absolutely ecstatic feeling in them. Even a few minutes of separation from the ground, just flying in the air, created a great experience of freedom. Even though that experience is momentary, it is a sign that in separation there is liberation. And in that liberation there is oneness, because even though you are flying and are totally free from the sky, from the ground, and from people, you know everything is right there for you. So both experiences, of liberation and of oneness, are combined in a single experience.

It is the same when we are falling asleep. We separate ourselves from everything and everyone, and there is a euphoric feeling. You are happy, and you know you are happy. You are away from the troubles of the world. You are away from the worries of yesterday, today, and tomorrow.

Many years ago, I had to have an anesthetic, and I remember I was very reluctant to have it. It feels as though you are putting all the senses to death. The doctor said, "Don't worry. You'll come back to your senses. You'll be fine." So I said, "All right." The nurse spoke to me as she gave me the injection, and continued to ask me, "What is your name, and what do you do?" I was trying to answer her, but it was as if I was leaving. I got slower and slower — and I was gone! I was totally gone, but I knew I was gone. I knew I wasn't there. The whole time they were operating on me I knew they were there, and I knew they thought I didn't know they were there.

As you turn within all the way and go into the state of meditation, an incredible thing takes place in this body — which is matter, which is dense, yet which is filled with Consciousness. Even if you become oblivious to the world, there is still Consciousness, there is awareness. There is separation from this world, from your own body. Yet this separation is not complete, because there is an underlying oneness or union.

This is the beauty of merging and becoming established in the

Truth. You are separate, yet you are not separate. You are one, yet you are not one. You are different, yet you are not different. You are the body, yet you are not the body. You are the mind, yet you are not the mind. This is why Vedanta says: *neti, neti* — "not this, not that." In this state, while living in this body, you are not bound by the rules of this body; you are totally free. The body becomes your servant, your helper, your assistant. If you want to sleep, the body says, "All right, we'll go to sleep." If you want to be awake, the body says, "All right, we'll be awake." The body assists you. This is why the saint Krishnasuta says:

> Your body is not an obstacle;
> It is your helper.
> So why do you hate your body?
> And why do you hate this world?

Your body assists you in knowing the Truth, in experiencing the Truth. So the *Vijñāna Bhairava* says:

> Practice this: Refrain from all thoughts
>   and from all notions.
> And as you become free from all this,
> The inner awakening takes place.

Once the inner awakening takes place, spiritual energy courses through your life, through all your activities. Then, while living in the body, you can experience great ecstasy.

The *Paramārthasāra* says:

> Just as a face appears clearly
>   in a spotless mirror,
> So in a mind purified by the Guru's initiation,
> The Self shines in all its splendor.

When the inner awakening takes place there is grace, and when there is grace you can see the Self, the Truth, the love of God in everything and in everyone.

If you put a crystal on the fire, it cracks inside. As long as you keep it on the fire, it continues to crack into tinier and tinier parts. The crystal is still whole, but on the inside it becomes fragmented and reflects the light like a diamond with many facets. In the same way, as the inner awakening takes place, the fire of Consciousness burns away all impurities, all negativities. You are still in the body, but inside, everything becomes Consciousness, everything becomes light. In the crystal you can see all the colors sparkling, and it is the same with this body. As it goes on burning in the fire of love, in the fire of Truth, it becomes Consciousness, nothing but Consciousness.

In his song, the great saint Brahmananda said:

> I received the grace of my Master.
> He took away the negativities of my mind.
> He gave me the inner awakening,
> And by taking away the delusion of my mind
> He has made me love everything and everyone.
> So many scholars have told me,
> "Love is this, and love is that;
> The world is like this, and the world is like that;"
> Yet I only recognized the Truth
> When my mind merged into the Truth.

So through meditation the mind merges into the Truth, and when it merges into the Truth, it becomes the Truth. Once it becomes the Truth, it can see the Truth. Then, every word of the scriptures becomes a reality, becomes light. In the *Mahārthamanjarī*, the sage says:

> The independent Lord,
> Who is pure and who is scintillating
>   with light,
> Shines through all the senses of this body.
> The whole world is shimmering
>   with the light of Consciousness.
> There is no word such as "world" —
> There is only Consciousness.

This is the experience we must have, the true experience of living, the life of love, the life of perfection. In the world of duality, we have to see Consciousness.

It has been so tranquil and serene here. This is a blessing from God. He has given us Nature and He has given us a beautiful place to live. He has given us a beautiful place inside also. Just as we can live in a beautiful world on the outside and be thankful to Him for that, we shall also have to become thankful to Him for the beautiful world inside. We can recognize this by turning within.

We will chant the mantra *Om Namah Shivāya*. Remember, these syllables are a vehicle to take us to the world inside. For the inner journey this sound is a great vehicle. Then, as we are sitting quietly, contemplate. Refraining from thoughts, drop all your anxieties and contemplate becoming lighter and lighter and lighter.

You have been wonderful listeners, truly wonderful. Take that quality inside also. You have given your beauty and cooperation to us on the outside, so now give it to yourself on the inside too, so that you will continue to have it, no matter where you go.

Once again, with great respect and with great love, I welcome you all with all my heart.

Sadgurunāth Mahārāj kī Jay!

No One Wants To Be a Disciple

South Fallsburg, New York, April 6, 1986

WITH GREAT RESPECT AND LOVE, I welcome you all with all my heart. Just being in the ashram, there is such support from the *Shakti*. No matter what happens, you feel you are being cradled in Her lap. No matter what goes on in your life, the Shakti is stroking your face and consoling you all the time, and you just sway in Her bliss. All this comes from *sādhanā*, the practices.

Over the centuries the sages have always done sadhana. They meditated, they devoted their time to God for hours on end, in the land of yoga, in Ganeshpuri. When we come to the Catskills, it is the same. The sages from the past, whatever tradition they belonged to, spent long periods of time in contemplation. And since Baba first came here, contemplation has been practiced regularly again, and meditation has gone on. Hundreds of candles are lit day after day in this ashram. I am not just talking about the flame that is lit within each person, but those on the outside also.

This is the power of the practices. As you do your sadhana, you imbibe the teachings automatically. When you do not do sadhana, all you want to do is become a teacher or a Guru. The poet Bholenath sings:

> Anyone can easily become a Guru,
> But what is very hard is to become a disciple.
> What I say is not false. I speak the truth.
> No one is ready to receive the teachings;
> But everyone feels clever enough to give teachings.

Baba sang from Bholenath's poetry all the time, and in Ganeshpuri he had me read his poems constantly. This particular song stayed in my heart quite intensely, and I could never forget it, particularly the beginning: It is so easy to become a Guru, but it is so difficult to become a disciple. Over the years I knew that Baba had some purpose for my life, and to a certain extent I also knew the purpose. I was to impart the teachings after he had given them to me completely. That was quite something to think about, to live up to.

Before I took *sannyāsa*, I went to Baba and said, "Baba, make me a promise. Promise me you won't give me sannyasa till you've taken everything unnecessary away from me." I spoke very strongly, and I knew I was putting my life in danger, so to speak, by approaching the Guru in such a bold way. But I was quite adamant. I really thought he was going to yell at me and say, "Out the door!" but instead he started smiling and chuckling. His feet were down and they were crossed, and his toes began to move . . . and I knew everything was fine.

I kept waiting for the answer "Yes, yes," and he kept looking at me with a lot of sweetness. Then he said, "You think I would do that without fulfilling your wishes? How can you have such distrust?" I remember that was the moment I realized, "Yes, if that's what you want, that's what the Guru gives. If you don't want it, the Guru doesn't give it." When it comes to the highest attainment, you have to want it, and then the Guru gives it. In every other part of the training of sadhana, even when we don't want a certain thing, the Guru gives it to us so that somehow we will learn to want it. But when it comes to the final stage, there is no forcing. There has to be complete longing, and then it takes place.

Everyone wants to become a Guru, Bholenath says; no one wants to become a disciple.

I went another time to Baba — once again it was close to the time of the sannyasa initiation — and I asked him, "Baba, do I have the grace to remain a disciple forever?"

Baba's answer was, "You can't be a Guru unless you are a disciple." Just one sentence, "You can't be a Guru unless you are a disciple." This is something Baba had said over the years. He said it in the West, he said it in the East. However, when you have asked the question yourself, you feel as if you have really grasped it. I never asked high spiritual questions of Baba verbally — always mentally, and the answers always came through hints. But here was my time and my chance, the crucial opportunity; either you take it or you lose it. And that was what he said: "You can't be a Guru unless you are a disciple." It was enough. As long as you know that the Guru knows, and as long as the Guru knows that you know, then somehow there is perfect understanding. Then, of course, the giving takes place.

Everyone wants to become a Guru, but it is so difficult to become a disciple. So many times people used to come up to Baba and say, "I want to take these teachings and tell the whole world about them."

And Baba would say, "No."

They would ask, "Why not? These are the best teachings! Everyone in the world should know them."

And Baba would say, "No."

"Why not?"

Baba would say, "You haven't imbibed the teachings. How can you tell them to the world?"

And the person would say, "Well! I mean, the teachings are there; I should be taking them to people."

"No."

But people would never listen to that "No." Here is where the relationship between the Guru and the disciple begins or ends. In Siddha Yoga, if you have not imbibed the teachings and if you impart them, you do not last long. This is the simple truth. This is how Baba set it up. First you have to follow the teachings, and then you can give them to others. If you are not following them and you try to give them, you are lost.

Bholenath says:

From a small child to an adult,
From an ignorant person to a scholar,
Everyone has become a teacher.
Everyone wants to give teachings;
No one is ready to accept the teachings.

It is such a surprising thing. Nature is constantly giving the teachings, yet no one goes to Nature to receive them.

Once a seeker went to a Sufi saint. He found him deep in meditation, so he waited. When the saint came out of meditation, the seeker said, "You were sitting so still! Incredible! Not a single hair on your body was moving. Such stillness!"

The saint just laughed. "I learned that from a cat," he said.

This is how great beings are. We think someone descends from heaven and gives them something. But they learn from this very world, from things that seem quite insignificant. What is a cat, after all? What is a dog? Yet the great beings have learned from the animals and from the birds. That is what Bholenath says:

> Look at the ocean, look at the river.
> They are both trying to tell you something.
> Look at the animals and look at the birds.
> They are constantly teaching you something.
> The things of this earth constantly give themselves —
>   whether they are trees or plants or creepers.
> There is so much to learn from all of them.
> However, who is there to learn?
> Bholenath says, I look around but I don't see any disciple.
> If you are a true disciple, then you learn from everything
>   and everyone.

Here is a story Baba told hundreds of times. Once it was *Ekādashi*, a time of celebration, and a lot of devotees had gathered around Kabir. He just kept weaving and weaving. Finally one of the people in the audience stood up and asked, "Who is a true disciple?" Kabir gave no answer. He kept on weaving. Again the person got up and asked, "Who is a true disciple?" Kabir didn't say; he kept weaving. The man asked a third time.

At that point, Kabir called for his disciple and said, "Kamal, come here." Kamal went to him and Kabir said, "Go and get some *prasād* for these people. It is a day of celebration and by this time they have broken their fast, so give them some prasad. And when you bring the sweet prasad, add salt to it."

Kamal went and brought the sweet prasad, added salt to it, and distributed it to everyone. Everyone took the prasad — but it stayed on their palms!

After a while the same man stood up once again and asked Kabir, "Who is a true disciple?" He really wanted to know.

Then Kabir said, "Kamal, come here," and Kamal went to him. Kabir said, "I have lost my shuttle. Get a lantern and look for it." It was noontime, so it was very light. Kamal brought the lantern; he found the shuttle and gave it to Kabir.

The same man got up and asked, "Kabir, for the last time! Who is a true disciple?"

Kabir said, "You still didn't get it? Kamal is a true disciple. Didn't

Kamal know not to add salt to the prasad? But I told him to. Didn't Kamal know he could just pick up the shuttle? He didn't need a lantern. But I told him to bring a lantern. That is a true disciple: one who has such humility."

We hear this and we think, "My goodness, but how can I tell that this is my Guru and I should listen?" At all other times you know who your Guru is, but when it comes to obeying the command, then you hesitate. "How do I know?" you say. Haven't you experienced that? The true Guru won't give you a command that should not be given; this is another test of a Guru. So when you get a true command from a true Guru, it has to be followed to the utmost.

Kabir was demonstrating the real nature of discipleship, but no one had the eyes to see. The same thing happened around Baba. He did not speak all the time about what a disciple should be. It was always demonstrated, it was always revealed, but not all of us had the eyes to perceive it, because we got caught up in external matters. Somehow we would put up resistance, and we were not able to see through our resistance. Nevertheless, the teachings are there all the time: the teaching about humility, the teaching about surrender, the teaching about acceptance and about following instructions as fully as we can.

No one is ready to receive the teachings. Bholenath says, I don't see any disciple around. So often we think we have to prove ourselves to the Master or to the Guru, but that is a very wrong understanding. You can never prove yourself to your Guru. Never. If you ever think you're going to prove yourself, then you will only fall. If you have any desire to prove yourself, you go astray, because that desire comes from the space of the ego, and not from the space of humility. Just keep following the command and the teachings, and they will make you worthy of being a disciple.

Bholenath continues:

> If one does not become a disciple at all
> And only becomes a guru,
> Then he has no capacity to learn,
> And he falls from the right path.
> The disciple who receives the teachings
> Also receives everything.
> Such a disciple becomes the Guru of all Gurus;
> He is the best in this world.

If you don't want to be a disciple, only a Guru, then the whole system shuts down. You close yourself off to everyone and everything, because you are not willing to be vulnerable. When there is no inner strength, there is a fear of being vulnerable to criticism, to others' opinions, to others' thoughts. And when you can't face anyone or anything, you just close yourself off from the whole world. When you do that, there is no flow of the Shakti, there is no flow of love between you and others. You do whatever your mind thinks is right, but you do not notice how your actions affect others. You become very selfish, narrowly cloistered, and this state weakens you completely, until you finally fall from the true path.

A disciple who receives the teachings receives everything. If you are not afraid, then all the teachings come and make their home in your body, in your being. When you are open, this is also an invitation to greater knowledge and to the awakening of all the inner centers. Such a disciple becomes the Guru of all Gurus, the knower of all knowledge.

Bholenath says:

> Of course it is very difficult;
> Only very rare beings become disciples.
> In discipleship there is total annihilation
>   of one's individuality.
> In order to become the vehicle for the teachings,
> You have to die.

That is the simple truth. When you are a true disciple, you have to give up all your personal desires; otherwise you are not a good container for the flow of the Shakti. The only desire of a true disciple is to serve humanity, God's creation, and to follow the Guru's command. Such a disciple has complete *vairāgya*, absolute detachment, and his mind is inseparably tied to the Guru's command. Yesterday when a student was giving the morning talk, she quoted from the *Guru Gītā:*

> Purify your mind by following the path
> Which is shown by your own Guru.

When you follow the command, you are purified automatically. When you follow the teaching, not with blind faith, but with absolute faith, you are purified. You don't even have to do anything.

Not doing anything is very difficult. Baba had a devotee whom he would sometimes ask to reprimand someone, but this man would feel sympathy for people, and he wouldn't give Baba's message to them in the way that Baba had given it to him. He would coat it with a lot of sugar. Of course, when you change the teachings, when you change the command — to whatever degree — the impact is weakened, because the aim is diverted. So when you receive a command, or when you receive the teaching, it is fatal to change it even a bit. Whenever this devotee delivered his version of Baba's message, people didn't get the point. Baba knew the message he sent should have full impact, and he knew very well how much impact that would be. He didn't release the arrow and then wait to see where it went. No — first he had the target in sight, and then he released the arrow.

So when you are carrying the teachings that have to be imparted, it is very important that you become a true vessel, and that you keep the vessel very clean. That is your responsibility. The Guru, out of his compassion, gives everything. He is like a kind father who doesn't doubt you. He makes sure that you are ready, and once you are ready, he gives it all to you. Then it is your responsibility to take care of it.

God has given us birth in this world, and now it is our responsibility either to make something out of this life or to waste it. This is where free will lies. A lot of people think that once you come to the Guru there is no free will, but somehow with Baba there was *always* free will. He gave you multiple choices so you could do anything you wanted with yourself. But the more you twist the teachings, the longer it takes to get to the highest.

It is very difficult to become a disciple, but once you become a true disciple, you become the embodiment of detachment, because your mind is inseparably tied to the Guru's command.

Bholenath says:

> Once you become a true disciple,
> The pride of your own identification
>   does not exist anymore.
> The Guru's word becomes the Truth for you.
> Then you become a devotee of the Guru
> In your mind, your actions, and your speech —
> In every way you are the Guru's devotee.
> You give your mind wholly to the Guru's command.
> When you do that, your mind becomes the Guru.

There is an aphorism in the *Shiva Sūtras*: *chittam mantraha*, "The basis of the mind is mantra." As you repeat the mantra, your mind finally becomes the mantra; it becomes the embodiment of Consciousness. In the same way, as you follow the command, the word of the Guru, your mind becomes the Guru; then there is no difference. A true disciple gives everything of himself to the Guru; only then can he be called a disciple.

> When you become the command itself,
> Then you have all the qualifications of a disciple.
> And once you become the teachings,
> Then you have firm conviction.

This is the key: firm conviction. If there is no firm conviction, you cannot play any role in this world. Everything in your life goes up and down — it rises and falls, rises and falls. When you don't have firm conviction, you attract the same kind of people; people with weak minds become your friends. But once you have firm conviction, then all the inner secrets are revealed to you.

I received a letter from someone in Ganeshpuri. She said, "Gurumayi, I once heard you say that you would talk about the last syllable of the mantra *Shivāya*, the syllable *ya*. I've been waiting and waiting and waiting." One day, she said, she was getting frustrated: "How long should I wait, just to know this one syllable?" She thought, "I give up. I totally give up," and her head started nodding.

Then her whole being began to vibrate with the sound of the syllable. As the syllable started to reverberate in her body, she began to receive all kinds of teachings. Out of this syllable came entire scriptures, great wisdom. When she woke up, she felt full. She felt realized, and she experienced incredible contentment. She walked around seeing all the flowers and trees, the earth, the buildings, and the people — everything and everyone — in the light of this knowledge.

When you surrender and there is firm conviction, all secrets are revealed from within. Then you are called a true disciple. Of course, we have to remember again and again that it is not an easy thing to become a disciple. It takes ages, centuries. It is quite disheartening, I know! But if you keep following the path, one thing after another will be revealed to you, and you will understand. Every time there is an opening, every time there is an awakening of knowledge, know that you have broken through one more barrier. And as this awakening takes place, as this understanding comes to you, you feel as if you have taken a bath in a holy river, so pure, so clean.

If you just keep following the path, if you just keep pursuing the teachings, different realms open up. One thing we have to understand is that even though it seems that we are living here, we are also living on many different planes of existence. This is not the only one. As we go deeper, as we surrender ourselves more and more to the Truth within, all these realms are revealed to us. Sometimes people have the vision of literally going through door after door after door. And it is a reality: there are so many planes of existence.

If this were not true, we could not possibly love someone all the time, or hate someone and overcome it. We would just keep hating and hating — but that does not happen. There is a time when our feeling changes. When we have an inner awakening, when we wake up to a greater realm within, that change occurs, and we are able to love those whom we used to hate.

Many people asked Baba the question, "If I meditate on my own Self, if I love my own Self, if I follow the teachings, can I also love my enemies?" and Baba always said, "Yes." When you meditate, a different realm opens up and you see what you are and what others are. When you have this recognition, you can love others as well as yourself. No matter how many bad things they do to you, your heart won't give up loving them. This is how it should be. As the Sufi saint said:

> When someone strikes my heart,
> The only thing that flows from it is love.

There should not be poison. There should not be hatred. There should only be love, and that love should be for the world's upliftment. The world has enough suffering, so we should try to give our best. We should try to give the highest. This can only happen if we have humility and follow the teachings.

When you repeat the mantra, Baba would say, don't repeat it for me. Repeat it for yourself. When you meditate, don't meditate for me, meditate for yourself. If you do it for yourself, you can also give it to others. But if you don't follow the teachings, if you don't follow the instructions, do not give them to others. If you do, they will strike you down.

Once again, always remember this: If you do follow the teachings, if you follow the instructions, then give them to others. If you don't, don't give them to others. Otherwise — and this doesn't apply only to Siddha Yoga — those spiritual teachings, those instructions, will bring about your downfall.

When that happens, you don't know what is going on. You say, "I have been spiritual for so long! Why do I have to suffer this?" You may have been spiritual mentally, but if you haven't been spiritual all the way through, then you don't have the strength to bear anything. You are weakened inside. And as you are weakened, you crumble. Then you need to turn once again to the practices, you need to follow the teachings, if you are once again to be in contact with grace.

So now we'll do the practice of chanting *Om Namah Shivāya*. And don't worry about the last syllable!

Repeat the mantra as if you have never repeated it before. Repeat the mantra as if it were the most cherished object in your life. Let it go on inside all the time.

And when you sit for meditation, hand everything over to grace. Don't try to *do* something. Don't try to prove to yourself that you can meditate. Just sit for meditation and offer one thing after the other to the Truth, to God, to the Guru. As you offer all this, you will become lighter and freer, and the moment that happens, you will go very deep inside, into a very deep meditation.

With great respect and with great love, I welcome you all with all my heart.

Sadgurunāth Mahārāj kī Jay!

The Light of All Lights

South Fallsburg, New York, April 8, 1986

WITH GREAT RESPECT AND LOVE, I welcome you all with all my heart. Have we ever asked ourselves what it is that makes us continue to meditate? What is it that keeps us going?

If you are lacking in enthusiasm for your spiritual practices, then, like a dry leaf you must fall from the tree of yoga so that others can have space to enjoy the *Shakti* of this universe. On the other hand, if you have a tremendous amount of grace, you are able to persevere. But for that tremendous amount of grace, for the roots to send you a lot of sap, you must have loved the tree very much.

In his book *Play of Consciousness*, Baba says that he kept meditating every day, and he looked forward to meditation, because every day he saw a new color and a new vision, every day he experienced a further expansion. And this new color, this new vision, this expansion, made him become more and more realized. Each day there was so much more to experience in meditation, so much more to experience in the awakening of the *kundalinī* energy.

Baba said so often, "Meditation is not to become like a log, but literally to become Consciousness itself." He said that it became so much more exciting as he meditated every day. There were times when he would have a lot of experiences, and then there would be times when he had no experience, yet he had such great enthusiasm, such a need to attain the final goal, that he kept going. He knew that if he could just pass by all these signposts, though they were exciting, he could arrive at the final goal. It was this, the final attainment, that made him look forward to meditation.

When you have a high aspiration, it keeps you going. If you only desire a little bit of this and a little bit of that, you are very weak in your meditation, and if there is some difficulty, you fall apart. When your goal is very high, you keep going. No matter what happens, you know there is something greater, something supreme: the Absolute.

One of the things that Baba described most fully in his writings was the experience of seeing the Blue Pearl. He watched the Blue Pearl expand and contract, grow brighter and duller; he saw it scintillate and explode. He talked so much about it. Every day it was a different song, every day a different dance.

This Blue Pearl held the secrets of the universe. It was everything. He talked about it coming out of the eyes and going inside again. He said: "Compared to the expansion of the Blue Pearl, the universe appears to be as tiny as a dot. When the Blue Pearl expands in this way, an extraordinary Blue Being manifests from its center. He has a form of the utmost beauty, but it is not composed of the gross elements."

The Siddha Tukaram Maharaj said:

That form is the embodiment of Consciousness.
The Siddhas proclaim that the Blue Lord
  pervades all three worlds.

In meditation every thirst is quenched, every desire is fulfilled. Desire is related to the senses of this body: The eyes want to see something beautiful, the ears want to hear something beautiful, the nose wants to smell a pleasing fragrance, the tongue wants to taste delicious food, and the hands want to touch something soft and cozy. So all the senses desire something delightful. As you go deeper and deeper, higher and higher in meditation, all these desires are satisfied spontaneously.

When you see the Blue Pearl, the desire for beauty is satisfied. "He has a form of the utmost beauty." Once you have seen the beauty of the blue Consciousness within, everything else is very beautiful also. For this reason, Baba often spoke about Zipruanna, another great Siddha. Zipruanna used to sit on a heap of garbage. Nevertheless, out of his body came a divine fragrance, because he had that amazing, continuous experience of this universe as Consciousness.

When you have this awareness, then everyone you look at is very beautiful: You see only beauty in everyone. But if you have not had this experience, whatever you look at, even the most beautiful palace, is very ugly. The vision of the Blue Pearl opens us and cleanses the center of beauty. The fact is that the only way you can see ugliness in someone else is when you have not experienced the beauty of your own Self within.

Baba said: "That Being, the embodiment of Consciousness, is made of extraordinary light — blue, red, and all the colors of the morning sun. He is a miraculous, radiant Being. In meditation, he stands directly before the yogi, before the meditator. There are no words to describe his beauty."

Jnaneshwar, a supreme Guru among Siddhas, called him the Light of Consciousness: *hechi ātmaprabhā nitya navi,* "The light of the Self is ever new." It is ever beautiful, ever bright.

This is why the sages have the tradition of making a chalk design called a *rangoli* in front of the house every day. It is made with different colors, the colors of the morning sun, and it represents the awakening within. Once the inner awakening has taken place, so many colors manifest themselves. Thereafter, whatever you look at has the color of the Self. Then, as Baba said, "the prescription of your glasses is correct," because the inner awakening has taken place and you are seeing through the clarity of the Self, not through the impurity of the mind. It is a beautiful awakening.

"Day after day," Baba said, "I looked forward to meditation, because every day the Blue Pearl revealed so many different things."

The Blue Pearl functions on many different levels. It opens up not only the center of beauty, but the center of hearing as well. Then there is a recognition: someone may be saying something to you, but you recognize that you have already heard it a million times before. And that is the case. We have been here so many millions of lifetimes. When the center of hearing is awakened, you recognize the actual words people are saying. The center of hearing also awakens you to whether what is being said is truth or falsehood. When someone is telling you a lie, there is absolute recognition of the fact. So, if you tell a lie in front of a sage, that lie strikes you down. For this reason, it is said in the *Guru Gītā,* "Don't tell a lie in front of the Guru." The Guru has that inner power of recognition. Through the vision of the Blue Pearl, through the vision of the final goal, his center of hearing has been fully awakened.

In meditation the same Blue Pearl, the same light, also purifies the center of fragrance. You begin to smell a beautiful fragrance from within. Often people say, "I was walking through the gardens of Ganeshpuri, and all of a sudden a whiff of beautiful fragrance came my way." Baba would always say to them, "This is the fragrance of the Siddhas that you smell. They are constantly walking everywhere in the gardens." When this center opens up within, you continually experience fragrance permeating your whole body.

When the center of flavor is awakened, whatever you eat, no matter how dry it is — even a rice cake — tastes delicious, and there is great sweetness to it. I remember when Baba used to have his meal, he would take a little piece of bread, without any butter and without dipping it into any sauce, just a plain piece of bread made in our bakery, and he would start chewing it and chewing it, and he would say, "Mmm, such sweetness. So delicious." And he would give us a piece. He would say, "Taste it. So good!"

I remember thinking, "No butter? Just plain?"

I would start chewing, and he would ask, "Doesn't it taste good?"

I would say, "Ye-es. It tastes like bread."

He would say, "No, no, no. Not like that. The *rasa* in it, the rasa makes it so sweet."

And day after day, he would give us bread. Once he got your number. . . . Luckily, I could recognize that his sense of flavor must have been awakened. I knew he was a Siddha; he had had the vision of the final goal and had become established in it. So even if our taste wasn't the same, that was all right. However, such a being also has the power of grace to awaken the centers within. And later on, it became a lot of fun: when he gave you a piece of bread, you could taste the sweetness in it.

The same Blue Light, the same Consciousness, the awakened power within, also awakens the center of touch. Then whatever you touch, however hard, is the touch of God, the touch of Consciousness.

So these are the works of the Blue Pearl; these are its miracles. And as everything is awakened within, great ecstasy is also awakened. As you taste the flavors, the nectar inside, as you hear the music inside, as you see the Blue Pearl within, as every touch becomes the touch of God, you become established in the ecstasy of the Self.

In *Secret of the Siddhas*, Baba writes:

> The Blue Being is the radiance of the perfect knowledge of divine realization. A vision of Him is considered to be the realization of the form of God. Although the Blue Being has a form, He actually is formless. This is the experience of the Siddhas.

He has created the universe, pervaded it, and assumed its form. He stands quietly for several seconds before a lover of the Guru. He walks around the meditating yogi and utters a few words. These words bring both sweetness and mystery. At this point the yogi is very near the state of Siddhahood.

The mighty one, the Blue Lord, the Sovereign of Consciousness, stands before the yogi who has received the Guru's grace and utters these words: "I have eyes in all my limbs. I can see every atom of the universe. All my limbs, my hands, my legs, and my head, as well as every pore of my body, can speak." In this way he addresses the Siddha yogi for a few more moments.

Baba always spoke about this and wrote about it so beautifully. *Play of Consciousness*, his autobiography, was written in Mahableshwar, a retreat place in India, because during the month of May Ganeshpuri gets very hot, like an oven, and for writing the book Baba needed a more open space and a very soothing climate.

Every day, whatever he had written was read aloud by one of his people. It was an incredible period of about twenty-four days. He spent hours and hours writing, and then for at least an hour someone would read out those pages. It was magical. The whole place had the Shakti of the Blue Pearl, and everywhere you walked, you would bump into Blue Pearls — so many blue dots. Until then, we didn't even know what the Blue Pearl was. And now you would just be walking through the corridor and there they were. You would go to sleep and there they were, not just one, but millions of them, hovering over you.

I remember one night. It was eleven o'clock, and at that time we went to bed by nine. I began to have a vision of millions and millions of scintillating blue dots, and I knew what they were because I had heard about them during the day. Then, suddenly, they turned into a ball of brilliant light. They all became one huge ball of white light.

I opened my eyes, and the whole room was lit up. I thought all the lights were on, because how can something that you see with your eyes closed still be there when you open them? When you have a dream and you open your eyes, it goes away — it's not real. I was totally perplexed. I went to turn the lights off, but they were already off.

My roommate, who was an older lady, asked me what I was doing. I said, "I'm turning off the lights."

She said, "The lights are not on!"

I said, "Yes, they are."

"Just go to sleep," she said.

I said, "I can't sleep while the lights are on."

She said, "Just go to sleep."

I tried to go to sleep but the whole room was lit up, and I could still see her sleeping. I said to her, "You know, this is really unusual."

She said, "What is happening?"

I said, "These blue dots have changed into a huge ball of white light and now the whole room is brilliant. I can't close my eyes because it's so bright. It is so bright that I can see you with the lights off."

She said, "You are hallucinating."

I said, "I don't think so."

She said, "You are hallucinating. You've been listening to Baba's book all day long. Just go to sleep." At that point I started having *kriyās*, so she got up and said, "Just cool down and go to sleep."

I said, "This light is making me have kriyas!"

This went on for two hours. Then she brought in another lady, and this lady believed in the experiences. She came and put her hand on my forehead and said, "Cool down, cool down."

I said, "Cool down? The light's on."

I think I finally fell asleep. The next day my roommate went to Baba. She didn't believe in any kind of experience or any kind of kriya, and she told him, "Baba, you shouldn't have your book read in front of these teenagers because they hallucinate after hearing your experiences."

And Baba was so happy with it. He started laughing and laughing. He told me, "Meditate for three hours instead of one hour, so you will be able to digest what is happening to you. It is the power of the Shakti."

And this is the beauty of this universe, and the beauty of Siddha Yoga. Inner experiences can happen anywhere, even on a heap of garbage, or with a person who doesn't believe in them. Somehow this light pierces through everything. At one stage, when you don't understand it, you may have a feeling of conflict. Finally, when you do understand it, it seeps through all the senses and the centers of the body. Then you are able to have the ecstasy of each experience.

Baba says:

> That which Kashmir Shaivism refers to as the supreme Pulsa-
> tion, Consciousness, or the mighty Shakti, is the One who utters

these secret words. Just as Consciousness expands, pervades the entire universe, and once again contracts, similarly the Blue Being, Consciousness, the Great Light, once again becomes the Blue Pearl, as tiny as a sesame seed, and re-enters the body through the eyes. It lives eternally in the *sahasrāra*. The great Kundalini yogi now becomes established in the seat of Siddhahood.

It is an incredible inner process. Baba said that the Blue Pearl is described in every song of the poets, yet it is not written about openly. It is usually alluded to in a few words and kept a supreme secret.

Jnaneshwar Maharaj, however, talks openly about the same Blue Pearl, the same Blue Light, the same awakening. He says:

> As I watched the Self intently with my own eyes,
> There was an endless stream of blue light.
> The Blue Pearl resides in the *brahmarandhra*,
> In the center of a triangle.
> This is the language of *turīya*, which one should know.

The Blue Pearl communicates the inner knowledge to us. Jnaneshwar says:

> The turiya state is within everyone.
> By the grace of Nivritti,
> The secret was instantly revealed to me.

Nivrittinath was Jnaneshwar Maharaj's Guru. In another *abhanga* he says:

> That deep blue Brahman, the moon
>   of the seventeenth day,
> That Consciousness which pervades the universe,
> Are all in the supracausal body.
> In the light of the flame of Brahman,
> One sees only one Being in all the three worlds.
> This supreme Self, the light of all lights,
> Resides in the Brahmarandhra.

The "light of all lights," the vision of all visions, abides in the center of the triangle. From there, the light pours down through the whole body. Once the body is lit with this awareness of the Self, with the knowledge of God, it becomes the temple of God and a divine shrine.

It is because of this experience that all the saints and all the great beings have said, "Look within. This is where you will find the Truth. Look within. This is where you will find everything."

So meditate and look forward to meditation, not just for one thing here or one thing there. Have a higher goal, the goal of the full attainment. If you keep your goal of spirituality very, very high, then there is no fall whatsoever. It is when your aspiration is shallow that you fall into pits of desire. If you are seeking a higher goal, you soar; you become lighter. You dedicate everything about yourself to the Truth; you are not distracted. The current flows in one direction, and it takes you to the Truth.

The scriptures say that this total one-pointedness is like that of an eagle. If an eagle sees its prey, it swoops down and pounces on it; it moves very gracefully, but it attacks very eagerly. The Truth is attained in the same way. So when you meditate every day, or every other day, or once a week, let that yearning for the attainment be there; don't keep your experience shallow. And whatever experience you have — small or great — let that experience pervade everywhere.

When you begin to go deeper, if you have been hiding a lot of negativity inside, it starts coming up. Those things don't need to be spread. Nobody else needs them. If it is your jealousy or envy or pride that is coming up, let it burn in the fire of meditation. Let it burn and become ashes and just blow away.

Finally, once all this has been worked on and you start going deeper, all the centers begin to open. Then there is only beauty, there is only fragrance, there is only delicious flavor, there is only exquisite music. And there is ecstasy, nothing but ecstasy. Let that ecstasy pervade your atmosphere, your surroundings. Let the inside and the outside become one and the same.

We will chant the mantra *Om Namah Shivaya*. The Blue Pearl resides in the mantra also. So as we repeat the mantra over and over again, the Blue Pearl expands within the mantra. Then there are no more syllables, there is only light. It is the same when you sit for meditation. Keep yourself very light. Keep yourself as light as Consciousness, as light as a feather. When you keep yourself light, everything is worked on much faster, and out of your own being you are able to derive the Supreme.

With great respect and with great love, I welcome you all with all my heart.

Sadgurunāth Mahārāj kī Jay!

A True Way of Living

South Fallsburg, New York, April 19, 1986

WITH GREAT RESPECT AND LOVE, I welcome you all with all my heart. This morning the Intensive meditation was all-pervasive; the vibrations of meditation were in every part of the ashram. I kept moving around, going up and down, up and down, because if I had sat down I would have been gone. So strong is meditation, so strong is chanting, so strong is your faith. And this power comes from the *sādhanā* of discipleship.

What are the necessary qualities for a disciple? In the thirteenth chapter of the *Bhagavad Gītā*, Lord Krishna goes straight to the point. He says:

> Humility, unpretentiousness, nonviolence,
> Forgiveness, uprightness, service to the Teacher,
> Purity, steadfastness, and self-control —
> These qualities make you a disciple.

If you read the scriptures and the philosophies, three terms recur constantly: humility, purity, and self-control. They say if you have these three, then you become worthy of attaining the Truth.

Humility comes first. The hardest task we face in sadhana is to let go of our pride, the ego, because no matter how much we think others are manipulating us, it is always just our own ego. Everything that we say or do is to please our ego. We are constantly trying to make it feel good; we are completely at its mercy.

All the scriptures say that you cannot serve two masters in one house. Who are the two masters? One is the ego, and the other is God. You cannot please them both at the same time, because they do not like the same things. They are very different! Either you serve your ego or you serve God. Kabir said:

> As long as I existed,
> I had not met my true Master.
> Now that I no longer exist,
> There is no more ego,
> There is only the Guru.
>
> The path of love is narrow.
> There is not room on it for both the ego
>   and the Lord.
> Do you want to drink from the cup of love
> And at the same time maintain your pride?
> Two swords have never been lodged in one sheath.

Kabir says that it is necessary to make a choice.

> The path leading to the Lord
> Is easy and straight,
> But you walk on it crookedly.
> O ignorant wretch!
> You do not know how to dance,
> So you complain that the floor is crooked.
> The path of love is narrow,
> But it is perfectly straight.

Only one thing takes us straight to the Almighty, to the inner experience, and that is humility. Letting go of the hard shell of the ego gives the true experience of God. When there is humility, there is love; and when there is love, there is humility.

Jnaneshwar Maharaj says this of humility:

> Just as the ocean, which is a storehouse
>   of limitless water,
> Swells to contain the water of many rivers,
> There is nothing which a true disciple cannot bear.
> He is not even aware of the hardships
>   that he has undergone.

The greatness of humility is that a humble person does not even know he has it. He is not aware of how many people he has forgiven and how much he has tolerated. This is why he can tolerate everyone and everything. If you keep an account of all your good actions, you will feel encumbered and burned out. But true humility takes no account of itself. A person who possesses truthfulness of this kind never brags about his life; he knows that everything happens by the grace of God, the Guru, and the inner Self. When you are truly humble at all times, you see whatever happens as a great lesson.

Once there was a king, Shah Jehan. One hot afternoon while sitting in his living room, he began to feel very thirsty. He clapped his hands for his servants, but no one came. However, he was so thirsty that he decided to get a drink for himself. He discovered that the water jug was empty, so he went outside and started drawing water from the well. Then his hands got caught in the wheel.

At that moment, he smiled and said, "O Lord, I do not even know how to draw water from the well! How great is Your mercy that You have made me a king!"

When you are truly humble, when there is love in your heart, you are able to have this kind of perception. When you are burdened with pride, then no matter what greatness comes your way, you can see only falsehood. You are not able to see divinity in your daily life.

There was a preacher who always thanked the Lord for everything. Every day he began his discourse by saying, "O Lord, I thank Thee for a great day!" Of course when his congregation heard the same thing again and again, they began to make jokes about it.

One Sunday two members of his congregation were walking together toward the place where he was going to preach. It was a terrible, rainy day, and the road was clogged with mud. They said to each other, "Every day he has been thanking the Lord for a great day. I wonder what he is going to say today."

They went in and took their seats. The preacher began his talk: "O Lord, I thank Thee that not every day is like today!"

When you have true humility and God becomes your whole life, you offer everything to Him. Everything is offered to one place, to one Principle, to one God. This is the sadhana of discipleship.

The greatness of the sadhana of discipleship is that it is a complete philosophy of life. It does not involve becoming someone else's slave or servant. It involves the way we conduct ourselves in every situation, in every circumstance, at every moment, with everyone. The sadhana of discipleship is the sadhana of life itself.

So the first requirement is humility. If there is humility, there is also discipleship. You must remember that it is easy to become a Guru, to become a leader; but to become a disciple is very difficult. It is so hard to be an ordinary person, but being a disciple is the hardest task of all.

According to Lord Krishna, the second requirement is unpretentiousness, which means not pretending to be anything but the true Self. Vedanta says, "Do not superimpose your false identification with yourself upon God, upon the true Self. Do not pretend to be something you are not."

We think of "pretending" as being like children: little boys like to pretend that they are girls and wear their sisters' dresses, and little girls like to pretend that they are boys and put on mustaches and beards. This kind of playful pretense is not what Lord Krishna is referring to. He is talking of something much deeper, of always appearing one way on the outside and being something else inside. Baba used to say that although the demon Ravana had ten heads, they all faced in one direction. You could tell where he was looking. But in a lot of people those ten heads face in all directions, so it is very difficult to tell what they are thinking and feeling, or what they will do.

We constantly pretend in this way. It is partly the effect of our upbringing. For one person we are a sister, for someone else a mother, for another person a brother, for someone else a father, for other people an uncle, an aunt, a grandfather, a grandmother. We have to play so many roles, and it becomes second nature to us. So we also start pretending when we come to the Guru, when we are before God Himself. We try to hide, and it does not work. This is why Lord Krishna says that lack of pretense is the quality of a true disciple. If you go on pretending, one day you are devoured, totally swallowed up by your own pretense.

The sadhana of discipleship chisels away this kind of tendency. The sage Patanjali says: *yogash chitta vritti nirodhah*, "Yoga is the stilling of the modifications of the mind." So many thoughts are always in the air. You can look up and grab one, and then another.

Someone has a thought. You take it and say, "This is what that person said? Hmm!" And you eat it!

You go and ask that person, "Did you say that about him?"

The other person says, "What are you talking about?"

"You did! That is why you are reacting like that!" But you aren't

148

sure, so you go to someone else. "She told me that he said such-and-such, but he said he didn't! What do you think?"

That person shrugs or makes a face, and you say, "Ah, you are hiding something!"

In the meantime, you have totally forgotten who *you* are. You are always wondering about someone else. By the time meditation comes around, on whom are you going to meditate: the man who said he said it, the man who said he didn't say it, or the one who contorted his face? Which one of the three are you?

This may be a very simple example, but it is the way we live. There is so much pretense in our life. We don't know what we really feel. We don't know what we are. We don't know where we stand about anything whatsoever. So in the sadhana of discipleship, we do self-inquiry: Who am I? What am I? What is it that I feel? What am I experiencing? What does all this mean to me? Where do I stand? As you do self-inquiry, the habit of pretense melts away.

Talking about this, Jnaneshwar Maharaj said:

As a rich man, overtaken in a forest,
    conceals his wealth,
As a girl of noble birth conceals her limbs,
As a cultivator covers the seed
    sown in the ground,
So a true disciple remains silent
    about his good deeds;
He does not boast about all the work he has done.
He is noble in the performance of duty,
    generous when occasion demands,
    skillful in discussion of the Self,
Yet at other times appears to be a madman.
The trunk of the plantain tree
    seems to be light and hollow,
Yet the fruit, when formed, is firm and sweet.
Clouds, easily driven before the wind,
    may look totally weightless,
Yet they can send down torrents of rain.

When you become free from pretense, no fear whatsoever remains in you. As long as you pretend, you are going to feel a knot in your heart, and your heart will flutter. You are going to feel as if you have

149

an elephant's foot on your chest twenty-four hours a day, as if you can hardly breathe or survive. The moment you stop pretending, the real you appears — and the real you is very loving, very pure, and very beautiful.

This is why when you first wake up in the morning, it is the sweetest time. There is no pretense. You have not yet dressed up in the clothes of pretense. You are easy to talk to, easy to be with. This is the state that is needed in a true disciple.

Humility, lack of pretense, nonviolence, noninjury. It is very easy for us to be violent through our thoughts. Often we might look quite mild on the outside; we may even talk about nonviolence. But it is inside, in the way we think and feel, that we need to become nonviolent.

Once again, we need self-inquiry: Am I thinking the right way? Am I feeling the right things? Is this a test? How should I respond toward it? This noninjury, nonviolence, is necessary in another way, too. When times are tough, we become too hard on ourselves. We must be nonviolent not only toward others, but toward ourselves also. So many people start thinking, "I've been so bad! I've been so terrible! That's it! I'm not going to eat anymore." And they start fasting, not even drinking a glass of water. There are people who walk on their knees for days on end until they bleed. This kind of *tapasyā* is unnecessary in a disciple. But you do need nonviolence.

Lord Krishna says:

> The mind, O Arjuna, is the mainspring
>   of all sensory activities,
> And it works through the senses.
> Whenever there is an impulse in the mind,
> It is expressed through sense activity.
> When harmlessness is well established in the mind,
> It spreads out as the fragrance
> Pouring out from the center of a flower.

We need to cultivate the kind of generosity that Lord Krishna describes, so in prayer we ask for nonviolence toward ourselves and toward others.

Of course, this teaching can be misunderstood. Particularly during Baba's time, parents would ask, "Baba, what do I do with my children when they are being very mischievous? Should I discipline them, or should I let God take care of them?"

Baba would always say, "Of course you should discipline them. It is very, very important."

Then they would become frightened. "Baba, how can you say that? Don't you have a sympathetic heart toward little children?"

Baba would say, "When it is time for discipline, you have to show discipline; and when it is time for love, you show love."

So nonviolence is essential. On the other hand, we should not become lazy. Disciplining the body is not violent; it is good. The *Katha Upanishad* says, "There are two kinds of things: those which are beneficial and those which are pleasurable. The mind is attracted to that which is pleasant, rather than to that which is beneficial."

Discipline is not pleasant, but it is beneficial. If we choose only that which is pleasant, it eventually leads to our downfall. Many people do not want to make sacrifices in the beginning. At the end they are ready to do so, but by then it is a little too late. If you go for that which is beneficial, even though it is not so sweet in the beginning, the end result is nothing but sweetness.

Through nonviolence, noninjury, you don't become lazy, either. You remain strong, but you still have sympathy and compassion toward yourself and others. It is said that if you are a true ascetic, a true renunciate, you are completely devoid of anger. If there is any trace of anger in you, you are called a scoundrel, not an ascetic.

There was a great being who was absolutely enlightened. One day everyone was talking about a *sādhu* who had come into town. The enlightened being went to see him; he bowed his head and said, "Praise the Lord." The sadhu asked him to come inside and take a seat. After he sat down, he said to the sadhu, "I want some fire."

The sadhu said, "I don't have any fire."

A little while later the enlightened being said again, "I want some fire, O sadhu," and the sadhu said, "I don't have any fire here."

For the third time the enlightened being said, "I want some fire, sadhu," and the sadhu shouted, "Don't you understand? Three times you have asked me for fire. I have told you there is no fire, and yet you insist upon asking me again and again!"

The enlightened being sat quietly. After a while he said, "O sadhu, I want some fire."

The sadhu could not contain himself. He leapt up and began to rant and rave. Then he got a stick and said, "Don't ask me for fire again! You are playing a game." Then he started to thrash the saint.

After ten minutes, the enlightened being said, "Thank you very much. I got my fire."

The sadhu could not understand. "What do you mean?" he asked, and the enlightened being said, "When I first came here, I smelled smoke. So I knew there had to be fire inside."

A great being will go to any extent to remove the fire of anger. After the sadhu realized he had all that anger inside himself, he completely dropped it. The greatness of a sadhu, of a monk, is that he can drop something once he realizes he has it.

This is a story of nonviolence. Even though the enlightened being persisted and persisted in asking, "I want some fire. I want some fire," his action was nonviolent. He removed all the violence from the sadhu. This is also the way the Guru works.

During his time, Baba would ask you the same question over and over, sometimes even for as much as five years. He would ask you, "What is your name?" Finally you would lose your identification. You would wonder what your name really was, because Baba had asked you so many times.

This was a great technique of Baba's, and it worked profoundly. Even though someone else gives us our name, we become very attached to it. Baba's method took away that attachment to one's outer name and identification.

I remember for years on end Baba could not remember my name. It was very short, just two syllables, "Malti." He would say to his attendant, "Go and get her — you know, what's her name." Sometimes I would be standing right there! The attendant would mention various names. Baba would say, "No, the one who translates for me."

Even to me he would say, "What's your name?" Or he would call me by someone else's name. But it was truly wonderful, because there is so much ego attached to a name. This was my name. Since Baba could not remember my name, it became dust. What importance does it have, this name?

I felt sure that when I took *sannyāsa* he would give me a name that he could remember. But it continued! After I became a swami, he started to remember my old name. He would say, "Swami Malti." I could not have any attachment to any given name, but only to one thing: to Baba's love, the love of God. Names and forms change, but that love never changes.

Great beings have a way of persisting. It is a wonderful technique, an effective scientific technique because it brings you closer to the Self, to love, to true discipleship. Once you can let go of this attachment, it becomes much easier to let go of many other attachments that we cannot give up on our own. So when a great being persists in this way, he is still being nonviolent. He has only one goal: to make us merge into the Truth.

Another of the requirements that Lord Krishna cites for a true disciple is *āchāryopāsanā*, "service to the Teacher." This is one of the best qualities. The whole of Siddha Yoga is built on *sevā*, service. So many people learned how to work after coming to live with Baba, in India as well as in the West. So many people who had never cooked, never swept a floor, never washed their own clothes or dusted a picture learned how to do natural work, instead of depending on something else or someone else.

Jnaneshwar Maharaj says:

> The service of a true disciple has no limitations
>   of time and space.
> When he is serving, he does not think
>   about day or night,
> Nor does he regard any service
>   as either greater or lesser.
> The harder the work the Guru gives,
>   the fresher and stronger he becomes.
> Even though the work given him by the Guru
>   may be greater than the sky,
> He completes it by himself.
> The moment he receives the Guru's command
>   to perform any task,
> His body outruns his mind,
> Competing with it to finish the work quickly.

When there is this longing, when there is this desire for service, discipleship comes automatically. It is there waiting for us. When this yearning is there, all *riddhis* and *siddhis* are at our service: all the ten supernatural powers attend us. They want to serve the disciple. This is why, when you put yourself completely into work, there is no fatigue. You can keep going indefinitely.

I saw this with Baba day in and day out for ten years. I remember during his second world tour he would go to give a public talk at five o'clock in the evening. He wouldn't come home until one o'clock, but at four in the morning he was ready to go for his walk. And we all had to be up, of course. So we would go for a walk and come back. He would take a shower and sit for meditation. Then there was breakfast, and then he would come to the *Guru Gītā*. Then he would meet people, then he would go for his lunch, again he would meet people, and then he would study his books for a while. Then once again he would go and give his talk and come back at one in the morning.

In the meantime, he did many other things. You can see the result of his work now, in all the establishments he set up. He gave and kept on giving. There was absolute, total service. There was complete one-pointedness. He always said, "My Guru asked me to do it, and that is why I do it."

With this kind of surrender, you are able to accomplish great things within and without, and you never lose your centeredness, your meditation. You never lose touch with the inner *Shakti*, the inner power, which is always present, always strong, and which refreshes you as though you were taking a shower in holy water. The wellspring of the Self is always there. If you remember this source, you never feel burned out. This is true seva, true service, *āchāryopāsanā*.

When the third Sikh Guru, Guru Amardas, was already one hundred and five years old, it was obvious that he was going to take *samādhi*, and that he would have to leave a successor. A lot of people were pining for that position. Very few people pine for the position of disciple, but little children and adults alike all want to be the Guru. So everyone wanted to take Guru Amardas's place.

He knew who he wanted to be the successor, but he was not going to make it easy. So he called them all and told them each to build a clay platform. Thinking their task was very easy, each one built a clay platform. He came and looked at them, and said he did not like any of them. They had to keep building and rebuilding their platforms, and finally they understood: "This man is senile. He is one hundred and five years old. He does not like anything. He's becoming altogether too fussy." So they gave up making the platforms, gave up the idea of becoming the successor, and left.

However, there was one boy called Ramdas, and he did not stop making the platforms. Guru Amardas kept telling him he did not like them, so he said, "All right," and he made another, and another, and another. All the people who had given up began to jeer at him: "Why are you still there? What are you doing? Guru Amardas is old. He's crazy."

Finally Ramdas said, "Say anything about me, but don't say anything about my Guru, because only he has the eyes to see the Truth, not you." And he kept doing the work.

Then one day Guru Amardas told him, "You can stop building the platforms. I am content with this one."

Then he made him the successor, and he explained to everyone else: "You all wanted my position. I understand that. But none of you had the ability to serve cheerfully. You wanted to serve only because you were going to get the position. You did not have the ability to serve out of joy."

There are many hidden meanings within this story. The reason you are asked to do seva is that there is a time when you start becoming pure and clean. You need that time for cleansing, for austerities. Moreover, if you can learn how to obey, then you can also learn how to obey Nature, and how to obey God, and how to obey your true inner intuition and inner knowledge.

We have to learn to be flexible. It is not so easy, because we are not in good practice. If we drop something on the floor, we wait for someone else to pick it up. We won't bend even to this extent. So you can imagine what a problem we are going to have in bending before humanity, before God, before the Truth.

True service to the Master leads to true discipleship, and in true discipleship there is every attainment. If you have a chance, you should read Jnaneshwar Maharaj's book, *Jñāneshwarī*. He has written very beautifully about his love for his Master, about how he wants to become everything for his Master. It is this desire, wanting to become everything for the Master so as to put yourself completely at his service, which makes you become the Master within. When you focus your mind on the highest in this way for a long time, you receive the state of the Master inside.

The next requirement for discipleship is purity. You might think that once there is humility, there is also purity, and this is true. However, we need to cultivate this purity through cleanliness of mind, speech, and body. All need to be cleansed, one by one.

I said before that we may be quite nonviolent on the outside, but what about our thoughts? In the same way, outside we might appear very clean, but what about inside? Do we feel clean? Do we feel worthy all the time, wherever we are? Do we have a constant experience of our own purity?

Jnaneshwar Maharaj continues:

> If the heart is not pure,
> The display of outer actions
> Serves only to deceive others,
> Like adorning a dead body,
> Bathing a donkey in a holy river,
> Sprinkling a bitter pumpkin with sugar,
> Hanging flags on a deserted and broken-down house,
> Pasting food on the body of a starving man,
> Laying gold over an empty dome,
> Or painting fruit made of clay.

If there is no purity inside, external purity is in vain. Inner purity comes about only through discipleship. When we are humble and unpretentious, when we become nonviolent inside, when we have a forgiving and upright nature, when we serve, then there is purity, which can also be called integrity. This integrity, and nothing else, holds us together. Inner purity is our strength, our solid foundation. And this will always be there, no matter what our outer circumstances may be. The whole house may be broken down, but the foundation will remain.

Discipleship is the purest thing. When you are a leader, your ego can grow. But when you remain a disciple, there is no place for the ego because you know that whatever happens, happens because of your Master's grace. You are doing nothing. The Lord is doing everything. When you are pure, your actions are untainted by thoughts. You keep them very clean.

A certain great king needed a new attendant so he called for ten of his slaves. To each he handed a goblet. Suddenly he gave the command: "Throw it on the ground!" They all obeyed. He asked each in turn, "Why did you throw down my precious goblet and break it?" "Because you told me to, Your Majesty," they replied, one after the other. Finally the tenth slave, whose name was Ayaz, said, "Forgive me, please forgive me." The king chose Ayaz. He recognized that this young slave had good understanding and great purity of heart.

Although he was chosen as a minor personal attendant, Ayaz was so clear, so honest, that the king soon made him Keeper of the Royal

Treasury. Many of the courtiers became extremely jealous. "Who is this fellow?" they muttered to one another. "I'm sure he is up to no good. He must be stealing the jewels and selling them on the sly."

This story soon came to be believed by many people, and they felt it was their duty to inform the king of what was going on. The king was very upset, and couldn't believe his ears — he had really trusted Ayaz. Nevertheless, he had to investigate. "What evidence do you have?" he asked. They replied, "He sneaks into the treasury and locks himself in there for a long time every day." The king went to a nearby room where there was a slit through which he could observe his treasurer.

Ayaz opened the door of the safe. Very carefully he took out not jewels, not gold, but the old ragged clothes that he had worn as a slave. With great reverence he put them on and looked at himself. "O my friend Ayaz," he said with tears in his eyes, "never forget for an instant that it is the king, your beloved master, who in his greatness and compassion rescued you. It is his trust that enables you to do his work. Always serve him faithfully, remembering you can never repay your debt to him." Then he removed the clothes, folded them, put them away, and came out of the room dressed in his treasurer's robes.

The king was so happy. He embraced Ayaz and said, "Thank you, my friend. Your purity and humility have given me a great teaching. May I never forget that King before whom we are all lower than the lowest, who in His greatness and compassion brings us out of darkness into the light of the Truth." From that day on, the king became a pure and faithful servant of the Lord.

So in discipleship, this purity is maintained. This is why over and over again Baba said it is so easy to become a Guru. It is easy to become so many things. But becoming a disciple and remaining a disciple is the hardest, because it takes a toll on your life. To be a true disciple, you must sacrifice your entire being. You are constantly hammered; you are constantly pounded; you are constantly kneaded. All this maintains the purity of discipleship. This purity is the greatest gift you can ever receive. It is the greatest treasure. Constant purity is the treasure in a disciple and in the sadhana of discipleship.

When Baba went back to Ganeshpuri after his second world tour, I saw him at the samadhi shrine of his own Guru. He lay down at the feet of his Guru and rolled and rolled and rolled on the ground. A lot of other people witnessed the same thing. Here was this great Guru, a great man, totally enlightened. He did not need to do anything. He did not need to reveal anything. He was what he was. But there he lay on the floor. There was no pretense in it, no show in it, because when he got up, there was no Muktananda. I saw these orange clothes walk by me and approach Bhagawan Nityananda's statue, but there was no one inside. I was puzzled and profoundly affected by it, because my eyes were open; I was not hallucinating.

This is discipleship — not being your little self whom you know and everyone else knows, but being the Truth. To be as transparent as this, you need tremendous purity.

God is clean, God is pure. The Self is clean, the Self is pure. But according to Vedanta, superimposed on the Self is the barrier of the body, referred to as *adhyāsa*. To overcome this barrier, to be totally transparent and to merge into the Truth, absolute purity is required.

One of the first times I saw Baba doing a full *pranām* to his Guru was in his own ashram. Baba did his prayers by himself, not in front of other people, so we were not aware of his practices, his prayers, and his daily *swādhyāya*. Nevertheless, one day in the early sixties, as he was leaving to go on tour in India, I ran to see him off. And just before I got to his car, suddenly I saw him at the temple of his Guru and I began to cry.

All this time I had known him as a great being, an exalted one. I feared him, I was in awe. When I saw him I trembled. Now I saw him with his Guru! And I saw in him what I thought *I* was feeling about *him*.

I saw him becoming small and totally soft. And though I was a very little child, and had no idea of the Guru-disciple relationship or about merging with the Almighty, no idea at all, I saw in Baba such purity and such an incredible amount of love that I just cried and cried and cried. I did not even know why the tears were welling up in my eyes. I did not understand anything. What I was seeing was beyond my knowledge, beyond my comprehension. But the power of love, the power of purity was there. It was so evident. Baba left in his car, and I did not even go to say good-bye. I did not know anymore to whom I could say good-bye.

When there is such purity, you become totally transparent. This is how completion takes place. Then, the sages say, there is no "you," there is no "mine." It is all one. This experience comes from purity and from incredible love. It comes from the Truth.

In discipleship there must also be steadfastness, constancy.

The mind of a steadfast person is not disturbed
   by the activity of the body,
The sky does not move with the fleeting clouds,
The North Pole does not shift with the movement of the stars,
And when travelers walk, the road itself does not move,
Nor do the trees leave their places.

Steadfastness. In discipleship there is this quality of amazing endeavor. No matter what happens, you do not waver. No matter what happens, you stand like a pillar in a temple, a witness, watching and supporting, yet neither affected nor involved. This steadfastness, this firmness, is very difficult to attain, even more difficult to attain than humility — because we are very, very impressionable. We are creatures of habit. Many times we say, "I love my family." But if someone says something negative about our family, we say, "Oh, I never realized that. So, my wife is this? My husband is that? My child is like this?" There is no steadfastness, no faith.

This little human weakness sometimes becomes very strong, and it can destroy our entire life. It isn't just a doubt. A doubt can be very healing. Not being steadfast is more than just doubt. When the tiles on a floor are well fitted, the floor is strong. But if there is a single crack in one of them, it becomes weak. In the same way, a disciple has to be steadfast. It is all right even if there are many, many thoughts, as long as they are all stable. On this floor you can build a strong house.

Once a saint visited a town in which there was a great devotee. Everyone went to see this saint. He was a *murshid*, which means that once you see him, you become liberated from all your sins. Everyone thought the devotee would be the first to go and see the murshid, because just a short time before, his own Master had died, and they thought that he would be looking for *satsang*, he would be seeking the company of another great being.

The whole town went to the great saint, all except this devotee. Finally the saint himself went to see the devotee and said to him, "Everyone talked to me about you, about how great you are, how you are one with God and with your own Master. I have wanted to see you. Why didn't you come to see me?"

The devotee said, "O lord, I did not come to see you because they told me that if I saw you I would be liberated. My murshid has just left his body. I do not know where he is, whether he is in heaven or in some other place. And I do not want to become liberated before I know where he is, because if I went to a place where he is not, that place would become hell for me. This is why I stayed away from you."

The saint was very pleased by the devotee's steadfastness, by his total love and total faith in his Guru.

You cannot serve two masters in one house. Either it is your ego, or it is God. The choice is very difficult, but at one time or another, we have to decide. There is no way out. Why did God make it like this? Only He knows! If we try to analyze it, we will be sitting here for the rest of our lives, and for many, many more lifetimes as well.

The only way we can stay on the path of discipleship is through self-control. As Lord Krishna puts it, you need humility, unpretentious-ness, nonviolence, forgiveness, uprightness, service to the Teacher, purity, steadfastness, and self-control.

> He keeps the two guards of the *yamas* and *niyamas* —
> the yogic restraints and observances —
> Alert in the castle of the body
> At the gateway of his mind.

In this part of his commentary, Jnaneshwar Maharaj gets a little technical. He says:

> In *mūlādhāra*, *manipūra*, and *vishuddha*,
> He performs the three yogic *bandhas* —
> *vajra*, *uddīyāna*, and *jālandhara* —
> And makes his mind enter the junction
> of *idā* and *pingalā*.
> He puts meditation to sleep on the couch of samadhi,
> And his mind, becoming one with Consciousness,
> delights in That.
> A person whose heart and mind silently and respectfully
> obey his every command
> Should be considered wisdom incarnate.

When water is steady, everything is reflected in it clearly. In the same way, if the mind becomes steady, if there is no movement in it, everything that is reflected in the mind is clear also. It is very difficult to control the mind, so a yogi puts forth a lot of effort to perform all these inner locks. However, this steadiness of the mind comes quite spontaneously in meditation through the grace of the Master. When these bandhas, these locks, take place automatically, the *kundalinī* energy moves very easily through the *sushumnā nāḍī,* the central channel, up to the *sahasrāra,* or the thousand-petaled lotus at the crown of the head. When the mind and heart listen to you, when they respect and adore you, know that you have attained discipleship, complete surrender and total humility.

In the *Shiva Purāna* there are beautiful descriptions of how a disciple should be:

> The Guru shall purify and consecrate the disciple,
> Either by knowledge or by means of rituals.
> A wicked person will perish,
> Therefore, the Guru shall test the disciple in every way;
> The disciple shall also carry out the Guru's tests.
> The Guru tests a disciple with regard to his worthiness
>   and his seriousness of purpose.
> The disciple shall endeavor to honor the Guru
>   in every respect.
> A disciple who seeks his own welfare
> Shall never think of disobeying his Guru's commands,
> Because only he who obeys his Guru
>   attains the wealth of knowledge.
> The disciple shall not do anything —
>   walk, stand, sleep, or eat —
> Without his Guru's permission.
> Especially if the work is performed in the Guru's presence,
> It must necessarily be done with his permission.

You might think this verse is quite extreme, but it is true. Around Baba we would not leave the room unless he said, "You can go now." We would not go and have our meals unless we had permission.

> Since the Guru is the Lord Himself
> And his house is the Lord's temple,
> The disciple shall not sit in any way he pleases
>   in the Guru's house or in his presence.

Of course, you should understand these things were written down by the sages after they had had the experience of the Truth. When you just hear about them, they do sound very strange, but when discipleship starts growing inside you, all these things arise automatically; it is all quite spontaneous. A beautiful verse in the *Shiva Purāna* describes it like this:

> Just as gold sheds its impurities when placed
>   in the fire,
> Similarly, the disciple sheds his sins through contact
>   with the Guru.
> Just as *ghee*, clarified butter, melts when placed
>   near the fire,
> In the same way, the disciple's sins melt
>   in the Guru's presence.
> Just as a blazing fire burns a twig,
>   whether it is damp or dry,
> Similarly, the Guru burns away the disciple's sins.
>
> If the disciple is intelligent and seeks his own welfare,
> He will never act falsely toward the Guru —
>   physically, mentally, or verbally.
> Whether he is asked to or not, the disciple shall perform
>   what is good and pleasing to the Guru.
> He shall carry out all his tasks.
> He who acts in this way, who is always devoted and alert,
>   and who pleases the Guru,
> Is entitled to the Shaivite rites.

When you please the Guru, he gives you many different kinds of treasures. The greatest treasure of all is that he gives you his state. He gives it to you inside; even if no one else can see it, you experience it. The *Shiva Purāna* says:

> The Guru is intelligent, endowed with virtues,
> Capable of revealing the inner bliss.
> Established in Reality and devoted to the Lord,
> He alone is able to grant salvation — no one else.
> Only one who knows the supreme Principle can reveal bliss,
> Not one who is a guru in name only but who lacks true knowledge.
> A rock cannot carry another rock across a river.
> If one is a guru in name only,
> Liberation will also be in name only.

The sacred texts say that disciples with
    the following qualifications
Shall be consecrated and enlightened:
They shall be nonviolent, merciful, always active,
    and alert in mind,
Free from arrogance, intelligent, free from rivalry,
    sweet-spoken,
Straightforward, soft-hearted, pure, humble, steady,
Pure of conduct, and well behaved in every respect.

The sadhana of discipleship is nothing but a true way of living. It is not becoming someone else's slave; it is becoming the master of your own life by obtaining the awareness of discipleship and remembering it constantly. When you remain aware of discipleship, your heart is totally molded into the absolute state. It is said that the heart of a saint is as hard as a thunderbolt but softer than butter, softer than a flower petal.

In the sadhana of discipleship you obtain everything that can be obtained. You become That. You become the Truth. Everything that we do is to mold ourselves into becoming a true disciple. One never becomes enough of a disciple. That is another glory of discipleship. You will never reach a point where you say, "Now I feel satisfied — I am a good enough disciple," "I am a great disciple," or "I am a divine disciple." Somehow that ideal is always there, but you have not quite attained it. You constantly aspire to it. Then finally, when you give up this body, *bhūyah syāt pratimīlanam*, the *Shiva Sūtras* say: "Shiva merges into Shiva; God merges into God; the Truth merges into the Truth." There is *pratimīlanam:* complete reunion, as spark merges into spark, fire into fire, water into water, the Truth into the Truth.

So we will continue our sadhana of discipleship. With great respect and with great love, I welcome you all with all my heart.

Sadgurunāth Mahārāj kī Jay!

Becoming Free from Everything

South Fallsburg, New York, April 20, 1986

WITH GREAT RESPECT AND LOVE, I welcome you all with all my heart. In the *sādhanā* of discipleship, there is a process of becoming free, free from everything and everyone. It is a process of elimination that makes possible a higher attainment. Until you have attained that freedom, you are stuck, to the point where you torture yourself all the time: If someone says something, it bothers you. If someone sees something in you, it bothers you. If something happens inside you, you are dejected. If something happens outside you, you are devastated. As long as you have not become free from everyone and everything, there is pain and sadness, and even though at times you feel joy and bliss, it is not a lasting experience.

The sadhana of discipleship makes you totally free. In this freedom, there is an incredible attainment. Living with everyone and everything, you remain happy, and when anyone asks you, "How are you doing?" you can always say, "I am fine!"

Yesterday I talked about Lord Krishna's statement in the *Bhagavad Gītā*, that humility, unpretentiousness, nonviolence, forgiveness, uprightness, service to the Teacher, purity, steadfastness and self-control are the qualities that make you a disciple. Once you have these qualifications, you automatically have the experience of being a disciple, which gives you the highest attainment.

Furthermore, Lord Krishna says:

He who hates no creature, who is friendly and compassionate,
Free from attachment to possessions, free from egotism,
Indifferent to pain and pleasure, patient,

165

Always content, self-controlled, and of firm conviction,
Whose mind and intelligence are fixed on Me,
Who is devoted to Me,
That yogi is dear to Me, O Arjuna.

"He who hates no creature." These teachings are found everywhere. However, when it comes to our putting them into practice, we always find an excuse: "Well, I can still hate this person." We feel it is our birthright to hate someone or something we don't like, and we feel a lot of self-righteousness in doing so. Nevertheless, over and over again we are told that if we want to experience humility and purity, if we want to see God, if we want to have the vision of the Truth, we must not hate any creature.

We must become free even from the word "hatred." What we hate, someone else might not. Someone we think should be hated is totally lovable for someone else. Similarly, we might like a person whom someone else hates intensely. We hate according to our own personal understanding. This is where we need to do self-inquiry. Why do we hate what we hate? As we think about this, we come to the deeper understanding: There is something within me that I don't like, someone within me I don't enjoy.

In this way, we are brought back to ourselves, and we are able to deal with the problem in a much better way. We realize there is no need to hate that aspect of ourselves. Then our hatred vanishes, and we are filled with love.

Once we recognize this part of ourselves which does not have to be hated or disliked, we very naturally become friendly and compassionate toward everyone and everything. A spontaneous flow of compassion, a feeling of forgiveness, arises within us. It isn't that we forgive others because we are *jada,* or dense. We forgive them because we have understanding.

Once this steady flow of compassion arises within, we are no longer attached to what we own or covetous of what we do not own. It is one thing to be attached to what we have, but most of us are attached to what we do not have. The biggest hurdle is to be free from attachment to possessions that we do not have. Greater and greater freedom comes with this understanding. When we are not attached to possessions which we do not have, then whatever we have has a greater value and brings about greater good fortune. Then we live in liberation.

There was a great king who earned his own living. Although he had many valuable things, after he had finished taking care of his subjects, at night he would go back to the palace and copy the Koran. The next day he would have his servant go and sell what he had written. He lived on whatever he earned in this way.

One day the servant received a letter from his family begging him to come back home. There was some kind of emergency to be dealt with. So the servant told the king that he must go home and that he needed his salary; he had not been paid for a long time.

The king told him, "I don't have any money right now. I can't give you anything."

So the servant waited. But he kept going back to the king, because he was still getting letters from his family saying that he must return. The king kept on refusing, saying that he had no money. Finally, three months later, the king gave him two rupees, which is much less than a dollar.

The servant asked, "Two rupees? Is that all?"

The king replied, "This is from my earnings. These two rupees will make you the richest man in the world, because I'm not attached to what I have in this palace. I'm not attached to anything that I don't have. This money is very pure; these two rupees are very clean. So take them."

What could the servant say to his own lord? He left with the two rupees. He had been working for the king for so many years. He wondered how he could go home without any gift for his family. They would expect something. "If I don't bring a gift, they won't be satisfied with me," he thought. "They will think I am a failure."

By the roadside someone was selling pomegranates, so he bought some, and got many more than he expected for his two rupees.

As he traveled on, he passed through a country where the queen was very ill. The physicians had said that she must have the juice of pomegranates, but in that country they did not grow them. So the king issued a decree: "If anyone can bring even one pomegranate seed, I will give him one thousand rupees for it."

When the servant heard the announcement, he immediately went to the palace with all his pomegranates. The king took every one and, as promised, gave one thousand rupees for each seed.

Obviously, the servant was now very rich, and when he returned to his family they were full of praise for all his great qualities. He had been serving the king for many years, and they felt sure that the king had given him all this wealth because he was so pleased with him.

All this came from just two rupees earned without attachment. This is why it is said: become free, become free, become free.

Yesterday someone said, "Gurumayi, I am an actor, and for my role I must smoke and display anger, yet the sadhana of discipleship is to make myself free from all this. How can I smoke and get angry and still become free?"

You do not lose anything through freedom; when you need something, it is there. Most of the time we have feelings that aren't even necessary. We get angry, but there is no one to get angry at. Still we burn with anger and jealousy and attachment, and we waste all our energy and strength. We feel totally burned out, weak, exhausted, and we receive nothing but bodily ailments. But in the freedom of discipleship, everything is there for us when we need it.

When you need something, if you are totally free you have the correct understanding of what to do to get it; you have perfect clarity of mind. If there is no freedom, there is no clarity either, because you are always acting on impulse and with limited understanding, not from a greater vision.

Through freedom, you become totally indifferent to pain or pleasure. Why should we become indifferent toward pleasure? After all, it sounds good! But pain and pleasure are relative to one another: If there is pleasure, there is pain; and if there is pain, there is pleasure. So if we enjoy pleasure, we should expect to suffer pain as well. It is better to become indifferent to both.

Kabir said:

> Become free from both virtues and sins,
> Because if you have virtues,
> When you finish them, then there are sins,
> And if there are sins, there will be virtues.
> Both sins and virtues become the cause
>   of birth and death.
> As you become free from both virtues and sins,
> You become free from both pain and pleasure.
> In turn, you become free from both birth and death.

Birth and death take place within all of us. At every single moment of our lives, we are taking birth and dying. Even our sleep is like a short period of death. This is why in ancient times they created the tradition of taking a shower after you wake up from sleep, just as after the body dies it is given a bath before being cremated or buried. It isn't only physical birth and death from which we must become free, but the birth and death that are going on within us all the time. When there is birth we feel inspired, and when there is death we are dejected. We become the puppets of inspiration and dejection. One moment there is a light shining from our body, and the next a ghost is crying out inside us.

But as we become free from birth and death, pain and pleasure, we also become patient. Patience, which can be called self-control, is the key to life and the key to sadhana. If we have even a tiny amount of patience, we can accomplish so much. There are times when, if only we could be silent, something great would happen, but we speak up and ruin everything. If we don't constantly speak up, if we have a little patience, greater things occur. Just by being silent, just by being patient, a space is created in which greater things can happen.

There is a universal force, the universal *Shakti*, which oversees everything. It is omniscient. It is omnipotent. When we become free from everything, we gain the patience to allow the Shakti, this universal force, to do everything.

To be patient does not mean to become lazy. I keep bringing this up, because it is very easy for seekers to think, "God does everything. The Shakti does everything. I don't have to do anything!" Then you become complacent and lethargic. Even though a lion can find its food very easily by sitting in one place, it doesn't just sit there with its mouth open. After all, no one is stupid enough to walk into a lion's mouth.

The quality of patience should become very natural, a matter of course for a disciple. You do not consciously say, "This is happening, so I'm going to be patient. I'm going to watch and wait and see what happens." Instead, patience should become the core of your being. Then whenever anything happens, you have the *ability* to be patient. Patience is not something you command yourself to do; it is a miracle that takes place within, through grace.

Patience brings about serenity and tranquility, and from serenity and tranquility still greater patience arises. All these qualities are interrelated. Each depends upon the other, and all exist together. If you start watching yourself, you will notice how bound or how free you are, and this understanding will enable you to become freer and freer.

Once in the *darshan* line someone gave me a toy parrot with a very long beak. There was a girl working in the kitchen whom we always teased about her long nose. All the time we were teasing her, she seemed to be happy and to take it very well. So when this parrot came in the darshan line, I said, "We'll take it to the kitchen."

We took it there. It was really a beautiful parrot, but this girl didn't find any charm in it. She got very upset and started crying. Someone said, "What shall I do?" and I told him, "Just make sure that she has it."

I left the kitchen and the man gave it to her. Later, at one o'clock in the morning, he found the parrot outside his door. So he took it inside and hung the cage by the window.

At 2 A.M. there was a knock on the door: "Give me my parrot back!" So he gave it back.

The next morning he told me what had happened. "Very interesting," I said. "I didn't realize there was a big parrot inside her that would hate a toy parrot."

It is always something very small which brings out a greater problem inside, so I said, "We'll just watch it unfold."

Time passed by, and after several weeks I received a very beautiful note from the girl, which said, "Gurumayi, I really want to keep the parrot. I have come to realize what it is inside myself I have hated for so long. The parrot has cleared up a lot of things inside me."

Many people write letters. Some people write them before they are completely baked. But that letter had such clarity and purity, you could see the light of patience. She had also really given herself a lot of time to go through the experience, whereas most of us want to get it over with right away. We want to quit; we don't want to go through the process of sadhana, because we feel it is very painful.

As we stop and look at ourselves, we are able to recognize what is happening, and we are able to let the energy do its work. We call it Shakti, we call it grace, we call it the power of *kundalini*, the power of the Self. Whatever we call it, it is the love of God. And the love of God literally does everything. It frees us from everything that we cling to, everything that prevents us from becoming greater and greater.

From patience arises the supreme wealth of contentment. This contentment allows you to accomplish everything. It is there when you are alone and when you are with people, when you hear pleasant things and when you hear unpleasant things. It is there whether you work hard or have less work to do. There is no greater wealth than contentment. It is full of love and peace. It is full of Shakti and awareness.

When you have a knot in your heart, you feel heavy, but when you have contentment you always feel light, and are always able to laugh. Lightheartedness and ecstasy are present no matter what is happening.

Self-control and firm conviction are also required of a disciple. Yesterday I quoted Jnaneshwar Maharaj, saying that the yogi obtains self-control through the inner *bandhas,* the locks in three different places in the body: at the base of the spine, in the navel, and in the throat region. This process gives great strength, because it holds inside what should be retained and expels what is not necessary for the system. It is a process which happens automatically through grace.

If we have the ability to offer and dedicate everyone and everything to the Shakti, to that great love, self-control becomes natural too. Self-control doesn't mean that you hold in anger, thinking, "I'm not going to get angry! I'm not going to get angry! I'm not! I'm not! I'm not!" This will only create an ailment, a disharmony in the body. On the other hand, the fire of yoga, the fire of meditation, naturally burns up all unnecessary emotions.

Whenever you are experiencing an emotional upheaval, just go and sit for meditation. Whether you are sitting with your back straight or you are cross-legged or lying down, close your eyes and go inside, and you will literally feel the fire enveloping you. This fire burns up all impurities. It is very difficult to get rid of garbage by carting it to the dump. It is much easier to incinerate it in the fire of meditation, in the fire of yoga, the fire of the Shakti.

Usually, if we are disturbed, we feel that we should talk to someone and sort it out. But that is not the way it works in the sadhana of discipleship. A disciple burns up everything in the fire of yoga. This is called self-control.

When conviction becomes firm, you have become totally established in the Self. What is the fire of yoga? It is nothing but the light of God, the light of the Truth. Once all your garbage is burned up, you become established in the Truth, in the light. Why must we meditate? Why must we see this light? What is the point of it all? It is so we can recognize this divinity within. Unless we recognize this divinity within ourselves, no matter how much we recognize it in others, it is of no avail. It has to happen inside. We must acquire this great state; we must give ourselves the privilege of having this experience.

"He whose mind and intelligence are fixed on Me, who is devoted to Me, is dear to Me." Once everything is burned up inside, our mind and our intellect are totally fixed on the Truth, on God. Then instead of God being very dear to us, we become very dear to God, and God worships the dust of our feet, the dust of His devotees' feet.

Once Narada wanted very badly to see Lord Vishnu. He had an urgent message to deliver to Him. The guard at the door said, "Lord Vishnu is busy. He is worshiping."

Narada wondered whom the Lord could be worshiping. He thought the guards were just fooling him. He waited for a long time. Finally Lord Vishnu finished His worship and came out. "Hello, Narada! What news do you bring today?"

Narada said, "Before I give You my news, O Lord, I must ask You, what were You doing in there?"

Lord Vishnu replied, "I was doing My worship."

And Narada said, "Impossible! How could *You* be worshiping?"

Then Lord Vishnu said, "I was worshiping the dust of the saints' feet."

"I don't understand," said Narada.

"If you don't understand," said Lord Vishnu, "go and ask a dung beetle about it."

So immediately Narada flew to the earth and found a beetle enjoying itself on a mountain of dung.

Narada said, "O Dung Beetle! What is the importance of the dust of the saints' feet?"

The dung beetle opened its eyes very wide and then closed them forever. No breath, no movement, remained. It had died.

Narada was shocked. He went back to Lord Vishnu and said, "The dung beetle died when I asked my question."

Lord Vishnu said, "Never mind. There is a beautiful baby swan in a nearby lake. Go and ask the swan."

Narada immediately flew back to the earth and asked the swan, "O Swan, I must ask you a question." The swan lifted up its neck, took a good look at Narada, and began to flap its wings; then it folded them forever and sank to the bottom of the lake.

Poor Narada went back to Lord Vishnu and said, "The swan died, too!"

"Don't lose courage," Lord Vishnu said. "A baby prince has just been born. Go and ask him!"

Narada said, "Lord Vishnu, the dung beetle had no relatives, nor did the swan. But the baby prince has a big family. If he dies when I ask the question, what will the king do? I will be in big trouble!"

Lord Vishnu said, "Narada, have faith. Do what I say." So Narada returned to the earth and entered the palace. Everyone was thrilled to see a sage coming to the palace just as the baby was born. It was so auspicious! They took him inside. The moment Narada asked the question, the baby prince was transformed into light. Narada was terrified.

However, the prince spoke. "O Narada, I had your darshan. I was touched by the dust of your feet when I was a dung beetle, and I became a swan. When I saw you again, I became a prince. And now I have become the Truth."

Narada went back to Lord Vishnu, bowed before Him, and said, "You have given me the answer I was looking for."

"He whose mind and intelligence are fixed on Me, who is devoted to Me, is dear to Me." In the beginning God is dear to us, but as we meditate and focus constantly on God, on this Truth, we become dear to God.

We saw this a lot around Baba. Of course we loved him, but it was so beautiful to see that he loved us in ways that we could never understand. It was always very moving when Baba would say, "So-and-so is working very hard. My heart goes out to that person." When you think of a yogi, you always think he has such a strong and solid heart. You never think of a yogi's heart as "going out." And when you hear that, you realize how soft and tender his heart must be, how incredibly beautiful it is.

Lord Krishna says:

> He from whom the world does not shrink
> And who does not shrink from the world,
> Who is released from joy, impatience,
>   fear, and distress,
> O Arjuna, such a being is also dear to Me.

We always think that the world is a burden on our shoulders, but we never stop to consider whether we might be a burden on this earth. But the earth, Lord Krishna says, is not burdened by a loving devotee. It blooms, it flourishes. Wherever such a person goes, there is prosperity. Wherever such a great being resides, there is an incredible wealth of love.

Such a person doesn't shrink from the world either, but accepts it in whatever form it comes to him. Many of us think that great beings collect only those who are good and reject those who are bad, and that therefore they lose touch with the world as it really is. For a devotee of God, for a true disciple, this is not the case. He accepts the world however it is, and through his power of love he brings about a transformation. For him, there is neither acceptance nor rejection. He embraces the entire world, and as a result the world does not shrink from him any more than he shrinks from it.

Many of us occasionally feel, "How I wish I weren't in this world!" or "How I wish I had a secluded place far, far away from this world in which to live."

Once I was watching the Miss America contest. They always have these shows just before the news or right after the news, because then they have your attention. The interviewer asked Miss America, "What would you like to do after this contest is over?"

She said, "I just want to live on an island all by myself!"

The interviewer said, "That sounds so good!" But he was realistic, so he added, "I don't think that's going to happen!"

Somehow this kind of desire is within everyone. She said it in front of millions of people, but we cultivate it inside ourselves. We say, "If I just had a place of my own on top of a mountain, I would never have to see this wretched world!" And everyone thinks we are meditating on the Truth!

Even people who work very hard for their livelihood cultivate this kind of secret desire. I met a man in California who is working hard because he wants to retire early. He told me, "I'm making all this money so that one day I can go and live on Kauai." He has two sons who are growing up.

I asked, "Who is going to take care of them?"

He replied, "Gurumayi, God is!"

So long as we are rejecting our lives in this way, the world is going to reject us. You must understand that whenever you hate something, that thing also hates you. So as long as you are thinking about running away from the world, the world also wants to run away from you. And if the world runs away from you, you'll be nowhere at all!

Therefore, in the *Shiva Sūtras* it is said, *lokānandah samādhi sukham,* "The bliss of the world is the bliss of samadhi." When you embrace the world, the world embraces you. Then no matter what is happening, the world gives you great support and love. God sends grace, and the world gives you its grace as well.

Commenting on this, Jnaneshwar Maharaj says:

> Just as creatures living in the water
>   are not afraid of the sea,
> Nor is the sea afraid of them,
> Similarly, such a man is not distressed
>   by the pleasure-loving world,
> And the world does not weary of him.
> Just as the body never tires of its own limbs,
> So he is never tired of any creature,
> Looking upon them all as his own Self.
> Because he experiences the world as his own body,
> He is free from all likes and dislikes,
>   from anger and joy.
> He who is thus free from the pairs of opposites,
>   from fear and desire,
> Remains devoted to Me always.
> Such a person is dear to Me, O Arjuna!
> He lives in My own being.
> He is content with inner bliss,
> And in him the highest Brahman dwells.
> He is the Lord of Fulfillment.

Drishyam sharīram, says one of the *Shiva Sūtras*: "This world appears to the yogi as his own body."

When you become established in love, you become totally free and start to live in the being of God. It is for this reason that the saints of all times have said with such conviction: "God's kingdom lies within." "I am Brahman." "I am the Absolute." "I am the Truth." "I am God." It is no longer just that God is living in your body, but that you live in God. Then, whatever happens is happening through the will of God, and there is total perfection.

The other day a man told me that someone had said to him that not everyone receives Shaktipat in the Intensive, just the chosen ones.

I said, "Oh, really!" and he said, "Yes, that's what I was told!"

This is the kind of thought that people love to entertain. It is impossible for them to understand that everyone really can receive Shaktipat. We constantly analyze things as far as our minds can go, and beyond that we say, "That can't be true. It is impossible." However, when you become totally free from everything, you realize that nothing can block the flow of the Shakti. The Shakti is ever-free. It is ever-playful. It is ever-awakened. It is ever-alive. It is so powerful that it can remove any kind of block. Even if you say, "My block is so big that the Shakti can't remove it," the Shakti will at least *sit* with your block. Then one day, when your block tips over, you feel, "How could I not have known all along that the Shakti was there?" So whether you think it is possible or impossible, the Shakti is awakened.

One day someone asked me, "Gurumayi, do you think I will ever attain God? I have no faith in Him." He was very serious when he asked the question. I said, "Of course you will." If God were to wait for us to have faith in Him, He would really be an old man! Just imagine if Baba had had to wait for all of us to have enough faith in the Shakti before he could awaken it! Think of how many lifetimes he would have had to wait. It would have been nice, because he would still be around. . . .

The power of this Shakti, this love, is such that it penetrates everything. This is the perfection and beauty of the fire of grace.

> He who is free from desires,
> Who is pure, capable, disinterested,
>   and free from anxiety,
> Who has abandoned all undertakings
>   and is devoted to Me,
> Is dear to Me.

Again and again in this sadhana of discipleship we hear the word "free."

> He who neither rejoices nor hates,
> Who neither mourns nor desires,
> Who has abandoned the agreeable
>   and the disagreeable,
> And who is full of devotion,
> Is dear to Me.

The line, "Who has abandoned the agreeable and the disagreeable," is very important. Our minds, our hearts, our intellects, and our beings are sometimes attracted and sometimes repelled, and we are caught in the middle of this attraction and aversion. Then we all disagree about what is agreeable and what is disagreeable.

I remember Baba quoting a song: "God exists in 'yes,' and God exists in 'no'. " If we allow ourselves to get carried away by what we agree and disagree about, there is no attainment. Once again, we must embrace both that with which we agree and that with which we disagree. In embracing both there is renunciation, and in this renunciation there is attainment. Then we find ourselves living in the being of the Lord.

> Alike toward enemy and friend,
> The same in honor and disgrace,
> Alike in cold and heat, joy and grief,
> Free from attachment,
> Indifferent to blame or praise, silent,
> Content with anything whatever, homeless,
> Steady-minded, full of devotion,
> That man is dear to Me.

"Homeless" and "steady-minded" describe the person who is free from everything, because the term "home" signifies our security, our base. When we become "homeless," when we have nothing that we cling to as our source of security, we are totally free. Many people resist any kind of change, but when you become homeless in your inner being, you have the ability to accept change. Once you accept change, you attain the fruit of sadhana immediately. Once you have the freedom to accept this kind of homelessness, then you can be anywhere and receive lessons. You don't have to be in an established place to experience the Truth. People often say, "I can meditate only in a cave, or only in the Intensive hall," but when there is homelessness, the Truth can be experienced anywhere and at any time.

Once there was a seeker called Malik-i-Dinar. He wanted to find a great Guru who could give him knowledge of the Truth. As he set out on his journey, he came across a dervish. He asked the dervish where he was going, and the dervish said, "I'm just walking. Where are you going?"

"Ah," said Malik-i-Dinar, "I am in search of a Guru who can give me true knowledge." The dervish listened to him. Then Malik-i-Dinar asked, "Do you know anything of this knowledge?"

The dervish said, "I don't know anything about anything. I'm just walking. If you wish to walk with me, you may join me."

Malik-i-Dinar said, "All right. I'll join you." So they walked on together.

In the course of their journey, they came across a tree. The dervish put his ear against the bark, and said, "The tree is telling me that there is a thorn inside it which we should remove, because it is painful."

Malik-i-Dinar said, "I'm in search of true knowledge! What do I have to do with this tree and its thorns? Let's get going!"

The dervish said, "All right," and they kept on walking.

Night fell, so they found a place to sleep. When they woke up in the morning, Malik-i-Dinar was very hungry. He told the dervish, and the dervish said, "I smelled honey in that tree. Let's go back and see if there is any honey there." So they went back and found a crowd of travelers, all eating great quantities of honey from the tree.

Malik-i-Dinar approached one of them and asked, "How did you know there was honey in this tree?"

"We didn't know," he said, "but we heard the dervish tell you that a thorn was hurting the tree. So after you both left, we removed the thorn, and all this honey gushed out."

"Oh."

The dervish and Malik-i-Dinar were hungry, so the travelers gave them some honey. They had their fill, and again set out on their journey.

They walked and walked, and soon they came across an anthill. The dervish knelt and put his ear close to it. He told Malik-i-Dinar, "The ants are telling me that there is a rock that is obstructing them from building their home, and that we should remove it."

Malik-i-Dinar looked at the dervish and said, "You know, I'm in search of the highest knowledge. These ants and their rock have nothing to do with me! Let's not waste any more time here. Let's get going."

"Very well," the dervish said. So they left.

Once again they made camp for the night, and when they woke up in the morning, Malik-i-Dinar said, "I have lost my precious knife! Where is it? I have to have a knife on my journey."

"You might have dropped it at the anthill," the dervish said. "Let's go back and find it." So they retraced their steps and came to the anthill. What did they find there? A crowd of travelers distributing gold coins.

Malik-i-Dinar went up to one of them and asked, "Where did you find the gold coins?"

"In the anthill," he replied.

"What?"

"Yes," he said. "We were walking by and we overheard the dervish telling you that a rock was obstructing the ants from building their home. Out of kindness we removed the rock, and under it we found a pot filled with these beautiful gold coins."

Malik-i-Dinar was amused by the whole thing, and the travelers were so kind that they gave some gold coins to Malik-i-Dinar and the dervish.

Then Malik-i-Dinar began to think: "Twice I missed out on something of great value. But what do I have to do with trees and their thorns, or honey? What do I have to do with ants and their rock, or gold coins? I am in search of the highest knowledge. I am going to find a great Guru." His ego assured him that all was well.

Once again they set out. They came to a riverbank and waited for the boatman to ferry them across. As they waited, a huge fish rose out of the water, and the dervish said to Malik-i-Dinar, "The fish is telling me I should feed him some herbs, because a huge rock is stuck in his gullet, and they will help to remove it."

Malik-i-Dinar said, "O Dervish, what do we have to do with this fish and the stone in its throat? I am in search of the highest knowledge. The boat has arrived. Let's get going." They sat in the boat and were ferried across the river. Night fell, and they lay down and went to sleep. Suddenly they heard a big commotion. They got up and saw the boatman coming, holding an exquisitely beautiful ruby in his hand.

Without wasting any time, Malik-i-Dinar asked the boatman, "Where did you find that?"

The boatman said, "Well, as I was coming to pick you up, I heard the dervish say that the fish was suffering. So, I fed it some herbs, and it coughed up this ruby."

This time Malik-i-Dinar got angry. He looked at the dervish and said, "All this time you knew everything! You spoke to me in riddles, and I couldn't understand what you were saying. I missed out on everything!"

The dervish patted him on the back. "O son," he said, "I told you, but you lacked the capacity to understand what I was telling you. You were seeking to learn from the greatest Guru, but you yourself have not taken the trouble to become even the smallest disciple! Until you become worthy through your own effort, you won't attain anything."

In that instant Malik-i-Dinar realized his folly; he became a disciple and received initiation from the dervish.

So when you become homeless within, you are able to receive teachings from everything and everyone, because you are more open and free. The freer you are, the greater your attainment. So many times, Baba would call people to tell them something, but they were not ready to understand what he said. Sometimes when he was giving talks, he would build up to a point, and then say, "You are not ready." And he would say something else.

If we are not becoming freer and freer, that shows that we are not ready. The whole point of sadhana, of discipleship, is to become free from everything and everyone.

Jnaneshwar Maharaj says:

Just as the sky is not tainted by its clouds,
Such a man is neither offended by scorn
    nor elated by praise.
Therefore, regarding praise and blame
    with equal indifference,
He either moves among men
    or remains in seclusion,
Free as the air.

Once again, the sadhana of discipleship is not to become a slave, but to become free from everyone and everything. All the elements of this universe are free, so we can learn discipleship from this universe. It is freedom which allows us to go inside very naturally and to function outside very naturally. Then we don't have to pretend when we meditate; we don't have to pretend when we are being active. We can be the true Self at all times.

When the scriptures say, "Be yourself," they do not mean, "Be your stupid self"! They are speaking of the higher Self, the true Self, the divine Self. Every one of us has this incredible beauty within. This is what we should be all the time. In meditation, we merge into this beauty.

As you sit for meditation, remember that meditation is not doing anything. If thoughts come up — regardless of whether they are loving or full of hate, arrogant or humble — simply let them arise and evaporate. Learn to detach yourself from them. When you are living with a Master, this happens spontaneously. Even though it is brought about quite naturally through service, Baba designed the Intensive to give us the opportunity to become conscious of this process and to be filled with the hope that we can make it a constant experience.

Practice detachment. There is no reason to cling to anything, because whatever we hold on to, imagining it as a support, is not really a support. We look for support in a person, in a thing, in a place, in a time, but none of these is everlasting. One day that person goes. One day you leave that place. One day that time has passed or that thing has disappeared. Then what? What are we left with?

We rebuild our hope, setting it on another person or another place, another time or another thing. When that, too, is swept away, then what? Once again, we rebuild hope. We think, "It can't happen again." But it does. It will happen without fail until we learn our lesson.

As you free yourself from everything and everyone, every place and every time, every planet and every star, every moment and every year, you feel a wonderful rush of ecstasy. In fact, you enter into another realm, an expanded realm of light and understanding. This realm is inside. Even though we may feel it is an out-of-the-body experience, it is within this body. It has just never occurred to us that such a realm lies right within our own body.

We repeat the mantra. We focus our mind on the breath. We focus our attention on one thing or another, whether in our body or above the body. All this is done to free us from everything and everyone, so that within this cage we can have total freedom, unwavering discipleship, absolute humility, an experience of complete fulfillment.

When you have this experience, you become aware that this body is not a barrier, not an obstacle. In this body there is honey. In this body there are gold coins. In this body there is a ruby. Kabir describes his Beloved as a ruby, so brilliant, so multi-faceted, so colorful.

The ruby represents the inner Self. It is our inner wealth. By detaching ourselves from everything and everyone, we get in touch with our own Self and the Self within everyone and everything. We are not involved, we are not affected, yet we are with everyone and everything. This is called love.

As you place your body on your meditation mat, know that you are free from your meditation mat. You are not attached to it at all. As you keep your body in one place, know that you are not attached to that place. It is not the place that gives you the experience of the Self. As you start meditating at a particular time, know that you are not attached to that time; this is not the only time you are going to meditate.

Even though you are meditating at this time in this place with a particular Guru, you are not attached to this Guru. This isn't the only time you have meditated. You have meditated before and experienced this great Shakti. You are not attached to this place, you are not attached to this time, and you are not attached to this Guru.

If all this is true, then you are not attached to your body either. Once you were a dung beetle. Would you want to be attached to that body again? No! Another time you were a swan. Your body was beautiful, as white as snow, with such graceful movements. You had so much pride in that body, but neither were you the swan, nor were you the young prince. If you were none of those bodies, how can you be *this* body? You are not attached to the place, you are not attached to the time, you are not attached to the Guru, nor are you attached to your own body.

When you are not attached to any one of these, what is left? Why do you meditate? Why do you live in this body? It is the play of Consciousness. Within this body, in this place, at this time, with this Guru, you can experience what you have never known before. To taste this beautiful inner life, you live and meditate. It is an adventure to go deeper and deeper within, higher and higher within, and constantly to come across extraordinary riches, unimaginable phenomena. Sometimes you find great love, sometimes great ecstasy. Sometimes there is deep sorrow, sometimes there is unbearable grief. Whatever it is, it is the play of Consciousness. Becoming aware of this marvelous play within, you become wholly free from everything and everyone. Then, wherever you take your body, you do it because there is such joy in it. Wherever you take your mind, you do it because it is so rewarding. Life is no longer a burden, nor are you a burden on this earth. Your existence is the delight of this earth, and this earth is a delight for you.

It is for this constant ecstasy and constant love that we turn within, plunging deeper and deeper, rising higher and higher. As we detach ourselves from everything, we get in touch with every cell, with every particle of dust, with this entire universe. As we experience this oneness, our hearts throb and pulsate with love and longing. This longing is the cry for the ultimate experience.

We will chant the mantra *Om Namah Shivāya,* the cry of the heart. As we sit for meditation, keep yourself totally detached. However long we sit for meditation, know that you are detached from meditation also. You are here out of love, nothing but love. This is the sadhana of discipleship.

With great respect and with great love, I welcome you all with all my heart.

Sadgurunāth Mahārāj kī Jay!

GLOSSARY

Abhanga
A devotional song in the Marathi language, expressing the longing for God.

Absolute
The highest Reality; supreme Consciousness; the pure, untainted, changeless Truth.

Adharma
Lack of righteousness; failure to perform one's proper duty.

Ahamkāra
The ego; the limited "I"-consciousness.

Akbar
(1542-1605) A great Moghul emperor who consolidated one of the most extensive Indian empires. His administrative skills, benevolent nature, and interest in culture and religion endeared him to his people.

Akkamahadevi
(12th century) Also known as Mahadevi Akka; an ecstatic poet-saint of South India. In her short life she composed many *vachanas* (devotional poems) in the Kannada language; these poems were often addressed to Shiva as *Chenna-mallikārjuna*, "The Lord White as Jasmine."

Allama Prabhu
(12th century) A great Shaivite saint of South India, also known as Prabhudeva, he presided over a group of *vīrashaiva* saints who completely rejected formal ritual. He composed many beautiful *vachanas* (devotional poems) in the Kannada language.

Aparokshānubhūti
(lit. "the perception of what is not invisible") A work on Advaita Vedanta by Shankaracharya, explaining God-realization as the immediate and direct perception of one's own Self by means of inquiry.

Arjuna
One of the warrior heroes of the *Mahābhārata* epic; a great disciple of Lord Krishna. It was to Arjuna that the Lord imparted His teachings in the *Bhagavad Gītā*.

Āsana
1) A *hatha yoga* posture practiced

to strengthen the body, purify the
nervous system, and develop one-
pointedness of mind; the *yoga*
texts refer to eighty-four major
āsanas.
2) A seat or mat on which one sits
for meditation.

Āshram
A community where spiritual
discipline is practiced; the abode
of a saint or holy man.

Ashtavakra
(dates unknown; lit. "bent in eight
places") A famous crippled sage
of the Indian epics who taught
King Janaka about the nature of
Reality. His teachings are contained
in the *Ashtāvakra Gītā*, also known
as the *Ashtāvakra Samhitā*, which
describes the path to liberation. *See
also* Janaka, King.

Ashvamedha Yāga
(lit. "the horse-sacrifice") In this
sacrifice, described in the *Mahābhārata*, a horse was allowed to
roam freely, followed by the
king's army. When the horse
entered a foreign kingdom, its
ruler could either fight against or
become an ally of the invaders. If
new kingdoms were acquired in
this way, the horse was sacrificed
as an offering.

Ātman
Divine Consciousness residing in
the individual; the Soul.

Austerities
1) Rigorous spiritual practices.
2) Abandonment of the pursuit of
worldly pleasure for the purpose
of spiritual attainment. *See also*
Tapasyā.

Awakening
See Shaktipat.

Ayurvedic medicine
The ancient Indian science of health,
still widely practiced, which is based
on the Vedic scriptures. It teaches
that good health depends on
maintaining an even balance of the
three elements in the body: bile,
wind, and phlegm.

Baba, or Babaji
(lit. "father") A term of affection
for a saint or holy man.

Bade Baba
(lit. "big father") The affectionate
name for Bhagawan Nityananda,
Swami Muktananda's Guru. *See also*
Nityananda, Bhagawan.

Bade Baba Mandir
A temple honoring Bhagawan
Nityananda, Swami Muktananda's
Guru. Located on the grounds of
the Shree Muktananda Ashram in
South Fallsburg, New York, the
temple, which houses a statue of
Bhagawan Nityananda, was
originally constructed by Baba in
1981. In 1986 a major reconstruction
was undertaken and the new
temple was dedicated by Gurumayi
with a *yajña* attended by thousands.

Banarsidas
(1586-?) A Jain writer and poet who
flourished in the time of Akbar,
Jahangir, and Shah Jehan. He wrote
his autobiography, *Ardhkathānak*, in
verse, as well as other books of
poetry such as *Banarsi Vilasa, Nam-
Mala*, and *Natak Samaya Sar*.

Bandha
(lit. "lock") A *hatha yoga* posture
which temporarily "locks" a specific

area of the body to retain the *prāna*, or life force. The practice of *bandhas* gives great strength to the body. In *jālandhara bandha* the chin rests between the collarbones, above the breastbone; in *uddīyāna bandha* the stomach muscles are drawn inward; in *vajra bandha* the anal sphincter muscles are contracted and drawn upward.

Bayazid Bistami

(d. A.D. 875) A Sufi saint of the Naqshbandi Order.

Betel nut

The seed of the betel palm tree, widely used in Asia as a stimulant and for its medicinal properties.

Bhagavad Gītā

(lit. "The Song of the Lord") One of the world's greatest works of spiritual literature, part of the epic *Mahābhārata*. In the *Gītā*, Lord Krishna explains the path of liberation to Arjuna on the battlefield. *See also* Mahābhārata.

Bhagawān

(lit. "the Lord") One who is glorious, illustrious, and venerable. A term of great honor. Baba Muktananda's Guru is known as Bhagawan Nityananda. *See* Nityananda, Bhagawan.

Bhajan

A devotional song in praise of God.

Bhakti

Devotion to God or Guru.

Bhakti Sūtras

The classic scripture on devotion composed by the sage Narada; also known as the *Philosophy of Love*. *See also* Bhakti Yoga.

Bhakti Yoga

The yoga of devotion; a path to union with the Divine based on the continual offering of love to God and the constant remembrance of the Lord.

Bhartrihari

A king who renounced his kingdom to become a *yogi*; a collection of his Sanskrit poetry, *Shatakatrayam*, deals with worldly concerns, spiritual ideals, renunciation, and the nature of passion.

Bhastrikā

(lit. "bellows") A yogic practice of controlled forceful breathing which purifies the body and stills the mind. *See also* Prānāyāma.

Bhīk, or Bhīkha Sahib

(1713-63) A poet-saint of Uttar Pradesh. Devoted to God from childhood, he left home at age twelve to find his Guru. The best known collection of his *bhajans* is called *Rāmjahaj*.

Bhoga

Worldly experience.

Bholenath, or Bhole Baba

(19th century) A poet-saint of Uttar Pradesh who established his *āshram* by the Yamuna River. He composed *bhajans* and a number of poetical works on Vedanta, including the *Siddha Gītā* and *Vedānta Chandāvali*.

Bhukti

Enjoyment of the world.

Bindi
A red dot worn between the eyebrows marking the location of the "third eye," the eye of inner vision or spiritual perception.

Bindu
See Blue Pearl.

Birbal
A brilliant wit and poet, and the friend and minister of King Akbar; he was killed in battle in 1586.

Blue Pearl *(nīla bindu)*
A brilliant blue light, the size of a tiny seed, which appears to the meditator whose energy has been awakened. The *bindu* is the subtle abode of the inner Self. *See also* Four Bodies.

Bondage
Ignorance of the divine nature of the individual soul.

Book of Wisdom
(Kitab al-'Ilm) The opening part of *Ihya''Ulum al-Din* ("The Revival of the Religious Sciences"), written by the Sufi philosopher Al-Ghazzali (1058-1111). In seven chapters he discusses the value of knowledge, the different kinds of knowledge, and the duties and requirements of teachers and students.

Brahma
The supreme Lord. In the Hindu trinity, God in His aspect as the creator of the universe. *See also* Shiva; Vishnu.

Brahman
Vedantic term for the Absolute Reality.

Brahmananda
(19th century) A saint of Rajasthan who lived in Pushkar, where he was a devout worshiper at the only temple in India dedicated to Brahma. He expressed his learning and wisdom in the form of ecstatic *bhajans*.

Brahmarandhra
The subtle energy center at the crown of the head at the upper end of the *sushumnā nādī*. When the *prāna* reaches the *brahmarandhra*, one experiences the state of total freedom.

Brāhmin
The highest caste in Hindu society; *brāhmins* were by tradition priests, scholars, and teachers.

Brihadāranyaka Upanishad
One of the most important of the Upanishads, from the *Yajur Veda*. It teaches the identity of the individual and universal Self, gives instructions on worship and meditation, and describes the steps of *sādhanā* according to the philosophy of Vedanta. *See also* Upanishads.

Buddhi
The intellect.

Catskills
A mountain range in southern New York State. *See* South Fallsburg.

Causal Body
One of the supraphysical bodies; the state of deep sleep occurs here. This body is black in color and the size of a fingertip. *See also* Four Bodies.

Center
See Siddha Yoga Meditation Center.

186

Center Leaders Course
A training program for Siddha Yoga Center leaders.

Chakra
(lit. "wheel") A subtle energy center, or nerve plexus, located in the subtle body. There are seven major *chakras: mūlādhāra, svādhishthāna, manipūra, anāhata, vishuddha, ājñā,* and *sahasrāra.* When the *kundalinī* is awakened, it flows upward from the *mūlādhāra chakra* at the base of the spine to the *sahasrāra* at the crown of the head. *See also* Kundalinī.

Chāndogya Upanishad
One of the main Upanishads, from the *Sāma Veda,* it lists and illustrates through dialogue and legend the three requirements of *dharma* (duty): to sacrifice or give alms, to practice austerities, and to become the student of a true Master.

Chidvilasananda, Swami
(lit. "the bliss of the play of Consciousness") The name given to Gurumayi by her Guru, Baba Muktananda, in 1982, when she took the vows of monkhood.

Chitta
The mind.

Chokhamela
(14th century) A poet-saint of Maharashtra, devoted to Lord Vitthal of Pandharpur. His *samādhi* shrine is located at the door to the Pandharpur Temple.

Consciousness
The intelligent, supremely independent, divine Energy which creates, pervades, and supports the entire universe.

Dakshinā
An offering or gift to the Guru or to God. Traditionally, whenever a seeker goes to receive the teachings or blessings of a saint, he brings an offering. More than a custom, this act of giving creates an inner space for grace to enter.

Darshan
Being in the presence of a holy being; seeing God or an image of God.

Darshan line
The line which is formed as people come forward to pay their respects to the Guru.

Dervish
An ecstatic teacher in the Sufi tradition.

DeVille
A hotel in the Catskill Mountains which served as a temporary *āshram* for Baba Muktananda in the summer of 1976.

Dhāranā
A centering technique described in the *Vijñāna Bhairava. See also* Vijñāna Bhairava.

Dharma
Duty; righteousness; religion. The highest *dharma* is to recognize the Truth in one's own heart.

Dharmadas
(1433-1543) A poet-saint of Bundhogar in Uttar Pradesh. He was a rich merchant devoted to conventional ritual until he was initiated by Kabir into the understanding that God is beyond image and form. He became a great disciple of Kabir.

Dharmaraja
(lit. "just king" or "righteous king")
1) The name of Yama, Lord of
Death. In the *Rig Veda*, he is
considered to be not a god, but a
king who gives the dead a resting
place. 2) A name of Yudhishthira,
the eldest of the five Pandava
brothers in the *Mahābhārata* epic.

Dhyāna
(lit. "meditation") A state in which
the mind becomes quiet and one
experiences the Truth.

Dīkshā
Initiation; awakening. *See also*
Shaktipat.

Duryodhana
The eldest son of Dhritarashtra,
and leader of the Kauravas in
their war with the Pandavas,
which is described in the
Mahābhārata epic.

Dynamics Course
A course on the dynamics of
Siddha Meditation, one of many
educational programs offered by
the SYDA Foundation.

Ego
The limited sense of "I," identified
with the body, mind, and senses;
sometimes described as the veil of
suffering.

Ekādashi
(lit. "eleventh day") A religious
festival; a day of fasting and
prayer observed twice each month
on the eleventh day after the new
moon and the eleventh day after
the full moon. In Pandharpur
during *Ekādashi*, millions of people
gather to worship at the Temple
of Vithoba.

Enlightenment
The final attainment on the spiritual
path, when the limited sense of
"I" merges into supreme
Consciousness. *See also*
Liberation.

Fallsburg
See South Fallsburg, New York.

Four Bodies
The physical, subtle, causal, and
supracausal bodies which are experienced, respectively, in the waking
state, the dream state, in deep
sleep, and in *samādhi*. *See also*
Samādhi; Turīya.

Ganeshpuri
A village at the foot of the
Mandagni Mountain in
Maharashtra. Bhagawan Nityananda
settled in this region, where *yogis*
have performed spiritual practices
for thousands of years. Gurudev
Siddha Peeth, the *āshram* founded
by Baba Muktananda at his Guru's
command, is built on this sacred
land. The *samādhi* shrine of
Bhagawan Nityananda, in
Ganeshpuri, attracts many
thousands of pilgrims.

Ganga, or Ganges
Flowing from its remote source in
the Himalayas down through the
plains to the Bay of Bengal, the
Ganges is considered to be the most
sacred river in India, and all the
land through which it flows is considered holy ground. Thousands of
pilgrims follow the Ganges back to
its source at the ice caves of
Gangotri every year.

Gītā
(lit. "song") *See* Bhagavad Gītā;
Guru Gītā.

Gopīs

The milkmaids of Vrindavan, who were the companions and devotees of Lord Krishna. The *gopīs'* devotion to Krishna was so complete that they saw Him in everyone and everything.

Gunas

The three basic qualities of nature which determine the inherent characteristics of all created things. They are *sattva* (purity, light, harmony, intelligence); *rajas* (activity, passion); and *tamas* (dullness, inertia, ignorance).

Guru

(lit. "from darkness to light") A spiritual teacher or Master who has attained oneness with God. A true Guru initiates seekers into the spiritual path and guides them to liberation.

Guru Gītā

(lit. "song of the Guru") An ancient Sanskrit text which describes the nature of the Guru, the Guru-disciple relationship, and meditation on the Guru. In Siddha Yoga *āshrams* the *Guru Gītā* is chanted every morning.

Gurudev Siddha Peeth

(Siddha Peeth, lit. "abode of the Siddhas") The main *āshram* of Gurumayi and of Siddha Yoga, and the site of the *samādhi* shrine of Baba Muktananda. Founded in 1956, when Bhagawan Nityananda instructed Muktananda to live in a simple three-room compound near Ganeshpuri, India, it is now a world-renowned spiritual center. The Ashram, encompassing 100 acres and with living accommodations for hundreds of people, is charged with the power of divine Consciousness. *See also* Āshram; Ganeshpuri.

Gurumayi

(lit. "one who is absorbed in the Guru") A Marathi term of respect used in addressing Swami Chidvilasananda.

Habib

(d. between 737 and 772) A Sufi, fourth in line from Muhammed in the Nimatullahi Order of Sufis. He started his working life as a usurer but was so moved by the suffering of his debtors that he gave everything away, left Iran, and became a disciple of Hasan of Basra. He originated the Habibiyya Order.

Hanuman

A devotee of Lord Rama who was the perfect servant. His form is that of a monkey with extraordinary strength. His story is told in the *Rāmāyana* epic.

Hari

The one who stills the fluctuations of the mind; the aspect of the Lord which takes away shortcomings and attachment to worldliness.

Hatha Yoga

Yogic practices, both physical and mental, done for the purpose of purifying the physical and subtle bodies. The goal of *hatha yoga* is to awaken the inner energy, or *kundalinī*.

Hatha Yoga Pradīpikā

An authoritative 15th-century treatise on *hatha yoga* written by Svatmarama Yogi which describes the practice of various *hatha yoga* techniques such as *prānāyāma*, *āsana*, *mudrā*, etc.

Hazrit Ibrahim
(d. between 776 and 783) A prince
of Balkh (now in Afghanistan). One
day, while hunting, he heard a
voice reminding him about death.
The impact was so strong that he
renounced his kingdom to lead a
life of poverty and asceticism.

Idā
See Nādī.

Initiation
See Shaktipat.

Intensive
A two-day program designed by
Swami Muktananda to give direct
initiation into the experience of
meditation through the awakening
of the *kundalinī* energy. *See also*
Shaktipat.

Jālandhara bandha
See Bandha.

Janaka, King
(dates unknown) A royal sage who
attained liberation through perfect
fulfillment of his duties as king of
Videha. He was a great supporter
of the doctrines of the Upanishads.
His Guru was the sage Yajnavalkya.

Japa
Repetition of the divine Name, of
the *mantra.*

Jñāna Yoga
The yoga of knowledge; a spiritual
path based on continuous contemplation and self-inquiry.

Jnaneshwar Maharaj
(approx. 1275-96; lit. "Lord of
Knowledge") Foremost among the
poet-saints of Maharashtra, he was
born into a family of saints; his

elder brother Nivrittinath was his
Guru. His verse commentary on
the *Bhagavad Gītā*, the *Jñāneshwarī*,
which he wrote at the age of 16,
is acknowledged as one of the
world's most important spiritual
works. At age 21, he took live
samādhi (a yogi's voluntary departure
from the body) in Alandi, where
his *samādhi* shrine continues to attract thousands of seekers each year.

Jñāneshwarī
Also known as *Bhavārthadīpikā*, a
sublime commentary on the
Bhagavad Gītā written by
Jnaneshwar. It was the first original
scriptural work written in Marathi,
the language of the people of
Maharashtra. *See also* Jnaneshwar
Maharaj.

John of the Cross, Saint
(1542-91) A great Spanish mystic
and poet. He wrote some of his
finest poetry while imprisoned
under harsh conditions for his
support of the reform of the
Discalced Carmelites of Saint Teresa
of Avila. His works include: *The
Ascent of Mount Carmel, The Dark
Night of the Soul,* and *The Spiritual
Canticle.*

Kabir
(1440-1518) A great poet-saint who
worked as a weaver in Benares.
His followers included both Hindus
and Muslims, and his influence was
a strong force in overcoming
religious factionalism. The *Bījak of
Kabir* is a collection of his poems.

Kahlil Gibran
(1883-1931) A spiritual poet from
Lebanon and author of *The Prophet*.
His poetry, written in Arabic and
English, embraces the three great

spiritual traditions of the West —
Islam, Christianity, and Judaism.

Kannada
The language of Karnataka State,
South India; Baba Muktananda's
native tongue.

Karma
(lit. "action") 1) Any action —
physical, verbal, or mental; 2)
destiny, which is caused by past
actions, mainly those of previous
lives. There are three categories of
karma: karma destined to be played
out in the current lifetime; *karma*
for future lives, currently stored in
seed form; and *karma* created in the
present lifetime. The first occurs
even if the individual attains
liberation in this lifetime; the other
two are eradicated when liberation
is attained. *See also* Samskāras.

Kashmir Shaivism
A nondual philosophy that
recognizes the entire universe as a
manifestation of one divine,
conscious Energy; a branch of the
Shaivite philosophical tradition
which explains how the formless
supreme Principle, Shiva, manifests
as the universe. Together with
Vedanta, Kashmir Shaivism
provides the basic scriptural context
for Siddha Yoga.

Katha Upanishad
One of the principal Upanishads
from the *Yajur Veda*. It contains the
story of the sage Nachiketa, who,
given a boon by Yama, the Lord
of Death, asks for the supreme
teaching of the knowledge of the
Absolute. *See also* Upanishads.

Kena Upanishad
(Kena, lit. "by whom") One of the
principal Upanishads, from the *Sāma
Veda*, which establishes that
Brahman is the supreme Reality
by whom the mind, speech, and
senses perform their functions. *See
also* Upanishads.

Khwaja
A Sufi Master.

Koan
A paradoxical question or riddle
given by a Zen master to a disciple.
By contemplating the *koan*, the
disciple goes beyond the logical
limitations of the mind to a place
of direct insight into Reality. A
typical *koan*: "What was your face
before your mother was born?"

Krishna
(lit. "the dark one," "the one who
attracts irresistibly") The eighth incarnation of Vishnu. Lord Krishna's
life story is described in the *Shrīmad
Bhāgavatam* and the *Mahābhārata*, and
his spiritual teachings are contained
in the *Bhagavad Gītā*.

Krishnasuta
(late 19th-early 20th century) Also
known as Baba Garde, originally
Khado Krishna Garde. An educational inspector in the Vijapur
District of the state of Karnataka,
he was a follower of Siddharudha
Swami and author of the *Gītāmrita
Shatapādi*, 100 songs summarizing
the *Bhagavad Gītā*.

Kriyās
Purificatory movements — physical,
mental, and emotional — initiated
by the awakened *kundalinī*. *See also*
Kundalini.

Kulārnava Tantra
A treatise about the Guru, the

disciple, the *mantra*, and different forms of worship.

Kundalinī

(lit. "coiled one") The supreme Power, the primordial *shakti* or Energy, which lies coiled at the base of the spine, in the *mūlādhāra chakra* of every human being. Through initiation, this extremely subtle force is awakened and begins to purify the whole system. As it travels upward through the *sushumnā nādī,* it pierces the various *chakras* until it finally reaches the *sahasrāra* at the crown of the head. When this happens, the individual self merges into the supreme Self, and the cycle of birth and death comes to an end. *See also* Chakra; Intensive; Shaktipat.

Kundalini Course

A series of presentations, periodically offered by the SYDA Foundation, on the mystery of *kundalinī.*

Kundalinī Yoga

The process of attaining union of the individual self with the supreme Self through the evolution of awakened *kundalinī* energy.

Liberation

The state of realization of oneness with the Absolute; freedom from the cycle of birth and death. *See also* Enlightenment.

Mahābhārata

An epic poem in Sanskrit, composed by the sage Vyasa, which recounts the struggle between the Kaurava and Pandava brothers over a disputed kingdom. It is a vast narrative which contains a wealth of Indian secular and religious lore.

The *Bhagavad Gītā* occurs in the latter portion of the *Mahābhārata.*

Maharashtra

A state on the west coast of central India. Many of the great poet-saints of India lived in Maharashtra. It is the site of Gurumayi's *āshram,* Gurudev Siddha Peeth. *See also* Ganeshpuri; Gurudev Siddha Peeth.

Mahārthamanjarī

(lit. "the flower of the Supreme") A short, 12th-century treatise on Kashmir Shaivism written by Maheshwarananda, in which he describes the process of creation, the immanence of God, and the means to attain Him.

Mahāsamādhi

(lit. "the great *samādhi*") A *yogi's* conscious departure from the body at death.

Mahāshūnya

(lit. "the great emptiness" or "void") The state of the formless Absolute, which is empty in the sense that it is without manifest creation. It is not a state of nonexistence, because it has the nature of Being, Consciousness, and Bliss.

Mala

(lit. "stain" or "impurity") The term in Shaivite philosophy which describes how the individual's experience of pure Consciousness is limited by identification with smallness, separateness, and a sense of doership.

Malik-i-Dinar

(7th century) One of the earliest

Sufis, a contemporary of Hasan
of Basra, and a disciple of Rabi'a;
he lived a life of complete
renunciation.

Manas
The mind.

Manipūra
See Chakra.

**Mansur Mastana, or
Mansur Al Hallaj**
(A.D. 858-922) An ecstatic Sufi poet
saint who lived most of his life
in Baghdad. He also journeyed
through Iraq, Persia, Gujarat, and
Kashmir to the periphery of
China. He was hanged as a heretic
for his pronouncement *Ana'l Haq*,
"I am God", which orthodox
Islam of those days would not
tolerate.

Mantra
Sacred words or sounds invested
with the power to protect and trans-
form the one who repeats them;
the sound body of God.

Mantra Yoga
The *yoga* of the divine Word, the
science of sound, integral to Siddha
Yoga. The path to union through
mantra yoga is based on repetition
of a sacred *mantra* and
contemplation of its meaning.

Māyā
The term used in Vedanta for the
power which veils the true nature
of the Self and projects the
experiences of multiplicity and
separation from God. The force of
māyā conceals the ultimate Truth,
creating the illusion that the real
is unreal, the unreal is real, and
the temporary is everlasting.

Mirabai
(1433-68) A queen and poet-saint
of Rajasthan, famous for her poems
of devotion to Lord Krishna. She
was so absorbed in love for Krishna
that when she was given poison
by vindictive relatives, she drank
it as nectar from Krishna, and was
unharmed.

Mudrā
1) Various advanced *hatha yoga*
techniques practiced to hold the
prāna within the body, forcing the
kundalinī to flow into the *sushumnā
nādī*; these *mudrās* can occur spontaneously after receiving Shaktipat.
2) Symbolic gestures and movements
of the hands which express inner
feelings and inner states, or which
convey various meanings such as
charity, knowledge, and fearlessness.
Many deities, saints, and idols are
pictured performing these gestures
granting their benediction. *See also*
Bandha; Shāmbhavī Mudrā.

Muktananda Paramahamsa, Swami
(1908-1982; Swami, lit. "a monk";
Muktananda, lit. "the bliss of freedom"; Paramahamsa, lit. "supreme
swan") Often referred to as "Baba."
Gurumayi's Guru and predecessor
as head of the Siddha lineage. Born
into a devout, prosperous family
in South India, he left home at 15
to begin his spiritual journey. After
taking vows of monkhood, he
traveled throughout India for 25
years, studying the major branches
of Indian philosophy and yogic
science. His spiritual longing was
not satisfied until he met the great
Siddha, Bhagawan Nityananda,
whom he had seen once in his
youth. Bhagawan Nityananda gave
him Shaktipat, spiritual awakening.
Nine years later, after intense

spiritual practices under his Guru's guidance, he attained Self-realization. Before Bhagawan Nityananda left his body in 1961, he transferred the power of the Siddha lineage to Swami Muktananda. Baba made numerous tours of India and three world tours, during which he gave Shaktipat to thousands of seekers, creating what he described as a "meditation revolution." A list of his many books appears on the next to last page of this volume. His *samādhi* shrine is in Gurudev Siddha Peeth, Ganeshpuri, India.

Mūlādhāra
See Chakra.

Mundaka Upanishad
(Mundaka, lit. "shaved"; from the *Atharva Veda*) He who understands the teaching is shaved of error and ignorance. This Upanishad speaks of the knowledge of Brahman and the need for a Guru, and also describes rebirth and liberation. *See also* Upanishads.

Nādī
A channel in the subtle body through which the vital force flows. The three main *nādīs* are the *sushumnā nādī,* the central channel through which the *kundalini* travels upward after awakening; the *idā* which is on the left side of the *sushumnā;* and the *pingalā* which is on the right side.

Narada
A divine *rishi,* or seer, who was a great devotee and servant of Lord Vishnu. He appears in many of the Puranas and is the author of the *Bhakti Sūtras,* the authoritative text on *bhakti yoga.*

Nasrudin
See Sheik Nasrudin.

Nityananda, Bhagawan
(?-1961; Bhagawan, lit. "the Lord"; Nityananda, lit. "eternal bliss") Often referred to by Gurumayi as *Bade Baba,* Swami Muktananda's Guru and predecessor in the Siddha lineage. He was a born Siddha, living his entire life in the highest state of Consciousness. Little is known of his early life. He came from South India and spent many years traveling in the South, for a time living in a cave not far from Kanhangad. Later he lived in the sacred region around the Mandagni mountain in Maharashtra, where many sages had performed fire rituals and done austerities. The village of Ganeshpuri grew up around him. Although he rarely spoke, spending many hours in silent ecstasy, thousands of people came to receive his grace. Often their questions were answered, without words, in the stillness of his presence. He left his body on August 8, 1961. Bhagawan Nityananda's *samādhi* shrine is in the village of Ganeshpuri, a mile from Gurumayi's *āshram,* Gurudev Siddha Peeth.

Nivrittinath
(1273-97) Elder brother and Guru of Jnaneshwar. He commanded Jnaneshwar to write *Jñāneshwarī* and the *Amritānubhava*. His *samādhi* shrine is in Tryambakeshwara, near Nasik in Maharashtra.

Niyamas
Daily observances recommended for the practice of *yoga,* such as cleanliness, contentment, and mental and physical discipline. *See also* Yamas.

Om Namah Shivāya
(lit. "I bow to Shiva") The "five-syllable" Sanskrit *mantra* of the Siddha lineage, known as the great redeeming *mantra* because of its power to grant both worldly fulfillment and spiritual realization. In Siddha Yoga, "Shiva" denotes the Supreme Self or Consciousness.

Paramārthasāra
(lit. "the essence of the highest goal") A short, 11th-century treatise on Kashmir Shaivism written by the great saint Abhinavagupta. In 100 verses, he describes the nature of bondage and the process of liberation through Shaktipat, the descent of grace.

Parvati
(lit. "daughter of the mountain") Wife of Shiva and daughter of the King of the Himalayas; a name of the universal Mother or Shakti.

Patanjali
(A.D. 4th century) A great sage and author of the famous *Yoga Sūtras*, the exposition of one of the six orthodox philosophies of India and the authoritative text of the path of *rāja yoga*. *See also* Yoga Sūtras.

Patanjali Yoga Sūtras
See Yoga Sūtras.

Philosophy of Love
See Bhakti Sūtras.

Pingalā
See Nādī.

Play of Consciousness
The spiritual autobiography of Swami Muktananda Paramahamsa (1908-82). Written in 22 days at Maha-bleshwar in May 1969, it is a work of illumination, charged with the spiritual power of its author. It is unique in its description of *kundalinī* awakening and the unfolding of the Guru-disciple relationship.

Practices
Activities which purify and strengthen the mind and body for the spiritual path; Siddha Yoga practices include chanting, meditation, *mantra* repetition, *hatha yoga*, and *sevā* (service). *See also* Sādhanā.

Prāna
The vital, life-sustaining force of both the individual body and the universe.

Pranām
To bow; to greet with respect.

Prānāyāma
A yogic technique, consisting of systematic regulation and restraint of the breath, which leads to steadiness of mind.

Prasād
A blessed or divine gift; often refers to food that has first been offered to God and is thus blessed.

Pratyabhijñāhridayam
(lit. "the heart of the doctrine of recognition") An 11th-century treatise by Kshemaraja which summarizes the *Pratyabhijñā* philosophy of Kashmir Shaivism. It states, in essence, that man has forgotten his true nature by identifying with the body and that realization is a process of recognizing or remembering (*pratyabhijñā*) one's true nature.

Pratyahāra
Withdrawal of the senses from their

sense objects; restraining the mind's outward-flowing tendency.

Purānas
(lit. "ancient legends") Eighteen sacred books by the sage Vyasa containing stories, legends, and hymns about the creation of the universe, the incarnations of God, the teachings of various deities, and the spiritual legacies of ancient sages and kings.

Rabi'a of Basra
(A.D. 714-801) A great Sufi poet-saint and mystic. She was sold into slavery as a child, but the man who bought her was so impressed by her sanctity that he set her free. She withdrew into a life of seclusion, and many disciples gathered around her.

Rajas
See Gunas.

Ram Tirth
(1873-1906) Born into a poor family in the Punjab, he became a distinguished professor of mathematics, but out of his longing for God withdrew to the Himalayas, where he attained enlightenment. He lectured on Vedanta in India, Japan, and the United States (1902-4). He wrote many beautiful poems in the Urdu language.

Rāmāyana
An epic poem in Sanskrit, composed by the sage Valmiki, which recounts the life and exploits of Rama, the seventh incarnation of Vishnu. The story tells of the abduction of Sita, Rama's wife, by the ten-headed demon king Ravana, and of Rama's victory over Ravana with the help of Hanuman and the monkey kingdom.

Ramdas
A sage in the *Rāmāyana* epic.

Rangoli
A design, usually geometric, drawn on the ground in front of a house in the colors of the morning sun, to represent the inner awakening.

Rasa
Nectar, sweetness. The subtle energy that gives the experience of pleasure.

Ravana
The ten-headed demon who captured Sita from Lord Rama in the *Rāmāyana* epic, and was finally defeated by Lord Rama.

Reflections of the Self
A collection of more than 700 verses on the spiritual life by Swami Muktananda Paramahamsa. They are poems of prayer, of teaching, and of love, and include instructions on spiritual practices and daily life.

Riddhis
Supernatural powers.

Rumi, Jalalu'd-Din
(1207-73; also called Mawlana, lit. "our Master") The most eminent Sufi poet-saint of Persia. He settled in Turkey, where he mastered all sciences at an early age and was a respected doctor of law. After meeting Shams-i Tabriz, an ecstatic wandering saint, he was transformed from a sober scholar into an intoxicated singer of divine love. His major works include the *Diwān-i Shams-i Tabrīz* (*ghazals* or love poems) and the *Mathnawī* (didactic poetry).

Sadgurunāth Mahārāj kī Jay!
(lit. "I hail the Master who has revealed the Truth to me") An exalted expression of gratitude for that which has been received from the Guru. Gurumayi says these words at the beginning and end of every program.

Sādhanā
Practices, both physical and mental, on the spiritual path; spiritual discipline. *See also* Practices.

Sādhu
A holy being, monk, or ascetic.

Sahasrāra
The thousand-petaled spiritual center at the crown of the head where one experiences the highest state of Consciousness. *See also* Chakra.

Samādhi
State of meditative union with the Absolute. *See also* Mahāsamādhi.

Samādhi Shrine
Final resting place of a great *yogi's* body. Such shrines are places of worship, permeated with the saint's spiritual power.

Samkhya
One of the six orthodox schools of Indian philosophy. It presents a systematic account of the process of evolution. Samkhya is a dualistic philosophy which views the world as comprised of two ultimate realities: Spirit (*purusha*) and Nature (*prakriti*).

Samskāras
Impressions of past actions or thoughts which remain in the unconscious and are stored in the *sushumnā*, the central nerve channel in the subtle body. They are brought to the surface and eliminated by the action of the awakened *kundalinī* energy. *See also* Karma.

Sannyāsa
Monkhood; also the fourth stage of traditional Indian life in which, after fulfilling one's worldly obligations, one is free to pursue the goal of Self-realization.

Sannyāsin
One who takes vows of renunciation; a monk.

Satsang
(lit. "the company of the Truth") A meeting of devotees for the purpose of chanting, meditating, and listening to scriptural teachings or readings; the company of saints and devotees.

Sattva
See Gunas.

Self
See Ātman.

Self-inquiry
The process of contemplating and reflecting on the significance of one's existence. Self-inquiry strips away the layers of illusion, bringing one closer to the experience of the Self within.

Sevā
(lit. "service") Selfless service; work performed with an attitude of nondoership, without attachment to the fruits.

Shah Jehan
(1592-1666) Moghul emperor,

grandson of Akbar, under whom the empire prospered greatly. Best known for the Taj Mahal, which he built as a mausoleum for his beloved wife.

Shaivism
See Kashmir Shaivism.

Shakti, Kundalinī Shakti
Spiritual power; the divine cosmic Power which, according to Shaivite philosophy, creates and maintains the universe. The immanent aspect of divine Consciousness. *See also* Kundalinī.

Shaktipat
The transmission of spiritual power (*shakti*) from the Guru to the disciple; spiritual awakening by grace.

Shāmbhavī Mudrā
A state of spontaneous *samādhi* in which the eyes become focused within, although they remain open. The state of Supreme Shiva.

Shankaracharya
(A.D. 788-820) One of the greatest philosophers and sages of India. He traveled throughout India expounding the philosophy of absolute nondualism (Advaita Vedanta). In addition to teaching and writing, he established *maths* (*āshrams*) in the four corners of India. The Saraswati Order of monks, to which Baba and Gurumayi belong, was created by Shankaracharya. His written works include *Aparokshānubhūti* and *Vivekachūdāmani*.

Sheik (Baba) Farid
(1167-1266) A Sufi saint and writer, born in the Punjab. Deeply religious

from childhood, he received initiation into the Chishti Order at age 17. His successor was the famous Nizamu'd-Din Awliya.

Sheik Nasrudin
A figure originating in Turkish folklore during the Middle Ages, used by spiritual teachers to illustrate the antics of the human mind.

Shibli
(A.D. 861-945) A famous Sufi mystic of Baghdad. At age 40 he became a convert to asceticism and a disciple of Junaid of Baghdad. His sayings (*Isharāt*) are acknowledged as classical Sufi teachings.

Shiva
1) In Shaivism, Supreme Shiva (*Paramashiva*) is the all-pervasive supreme Reality, the unmoving, transcendent, divine Consciousness. 2) In the Hindu trinity, Shiva is the aspect of God as the destroyer of ignorance. *See also* Brahma; Vishnu.

Shiva Purāna
An ancient collection of legends about Shiva; a *mahā* or "great" Purana, it describes the origin and dissolution of the universe, its different ages, and the genealogies and deeds of famous kings. It also expounds Shaivite rituals and practices, including the means for attaining union with Shiva, or God.

Shiva Samhitā
A Sanskrit text on *yoga* in which Ishwara, the Lord, describes the correspondence of the universe to the human body, explaining how the practices of *hatha yoga* (*āsana*, *prānāyāma*, and *mudrā*) and of *mantra yoga* may be used to awaken

the *kundalini*, or inner spiritual force. *See also* Kundalini.

Shiva Sūtras
A Sanskrit text which Shiva revealed to the 9th-century sage Vasugupta-charya. It consists of 77 *sūtras* or aphorisms, which according to tradition were found inscribed on a rock in Kashmir. The *Shiva Sūtras* are the scriptural authority for the philosophical school known as Kashmir Shaivism. *See also* Kashmir Shaivism.

Shrī Vidyā Antar Yāga
A treatise which deals with the inner worship of the Goddess Kundalini by means of visualizations, *mudrās, mantras,* etc.

Shrīmad Bhāgavatam
Mythological literature composed by the sage Vyasa. This popular devotional scripture contains legends and stories of the life and teachings of Lord Krishna.

Shvetāshvatara Upanishad
One of the major Upanishads, from the *Yajur Veda,* in which the sage Shvetashvatara speaks of Brahman in its manifest aspect. *See also* Upanishads.

Siddha
A perfected *yogi*. One who has attained the state of unity-consciousness, or enlightenment. *See also* Enlightenment.

Siddha Meditation
Spontaneous meditation based on the awakening of the inner energy by a Siddha Master.

Siddha Yoga
The path to union of the individual with the Divine, which begins with Shaktipat, the inner awakening by the grace of a Siddha Guru. Guru-mayi is the living Master of this path. Siddha Yoga is known as the *mahā yoga*, the great *yoga*, and includes all the branches of *yoga*.

Siddha Yoga Meditation Center
A place where people gather to practice Siddha Meditation. There are over 600 Siddha Yoga Centers around the world.

Siddhis
Supernatural powers.

Sikh
Follower of the teachings of Guru Nanak (1469-1538), a Master who traveled widely, teaching liberal religious and social doctrines.

Sita
The beloved wife of Lord Rama. The story of her capture by the demon Ravana and eventual rescue by the monkey Hanuman is told in the *Rāmāyana* epic.

Socrates
(469-399 B.C.) A philosopher and mystic who lived in Athens and who spent his time in philosophical discussion; many young men were drawn to his teachings. As a result of his challenging attitude he was accused of subversion, tried, and condemned to death. His life, his teachings, and his death were recorded by his leading disciple, Plato.

So'ham
(lit. "I am That") The natural sound vibration of the Self, which occurs spontaneously with each incoming and outgoing breath. By becoming aware of *So'ham*, a seeker experiences the identity between his

individual self and the supreme Self.

Sohira, or Soyara
(14th century) A saint and the devoted wife of the saint Chokhamela of Pandharpur; sister of Banka Mahar and mother of Karmamela, who were also saints. She wrote many *abhangas,* devotional songs.

South Fallsburg, New York
The location of the Siddha Meditation Ashram which Baba Muktananda established as international headquarters of the SYDA Foundation in 1979. Since that time it has expanded to encompass three major residential facilities accommodating thousands of visitors who come to spend time with Gurumayi each summer.

Spanda Kārikās
A 9th-century collection of 53 verses composed by Vasuguptacharya. An important work of Kashmir Shaivism, it elucidates the *Shiva Sūtras* and describes how the *yogi* who remains alert can perceive the divine Principle in daily life. *See also* Shiva Sūtras.

Sūfī
One who practices Sufism, the mystical path of love in the Islamic tradition.

Sundardas
(1596-1689) A renowned poet-saint born in Rajasthan. The main collection of his *bhajans* in Hindi is the *Sundar Granthavāti.*

Supracausal body
See Four Bodies.

Sushumnā Nādī
See Nādī.

Swādhyāya
The regular, disciplined practice of chanting and recitation of spiritual texts.

Swāhā
(lit. "It is offered") A *mantra* used when offering oblations to the sacrificial fire. *See also* Yajña.

Swāmi or Swāmiji
A term of respectful address for a *sannyāsin,* a monk.

Tamas
See Gunas.

Tapasyā
(lit. "heat") Austerities; also the experience of heat which occurs during the process of practicing *yoga.* The heat is generated by friction between the mind and heart, between the senses and renunciation. It is said that this heat, called "the fire of *yoga,*" burns up all the impurities that lie between the seeker and the experience of the Truth.

Tat tvam asi
(lit. "Thou art That") One of the four *mahāvākyas* ("great statements") from the Upanishads; it asserts the identity of the individual self and the supreme Self.

The Touch
One of the four ways in which Shaktipat is given, the other three being look, thought, and will. During an Intensive, Gurumayi uses one or more of these methods to awaken the *kundalinī. See also* Shaktipat.

Tukaram Maharaj
(1608-50) A great householder poet-

saint of Maharashtra. He received initiation in a dream and wrote thousands of *abhangas*, devotional songs, describing his spiritual experiences, his realization, and the glory of the divine Name.

Tulsidas
(1532-1623) A poet-saint from North India, author of the *Rāma Charitā-mānasa*, which is the life story of Lord Rama written in Hindi, still one of the most popular scriptures in India.

Turīya
The fourth state of Consciousness, beyond the waking, dream, and deep sleep states. The *turīya* state is the state of *samādhi*, the state of deep meditation. *See also* Four Bodies.

Uddīyāna bandha
See Bandha.

Upanishads
(lit. "sitting close to") The teachings of the ancient sages of India. These scriptures constitute the "end" or "final understanding" (*anta*) of the Vedas, hence *Vedānta*. The central teaching of the Upanishads is that the Self is the same as Brahman, the Absolute, and the goal of life is the realization of oneness with Brahman. *See also* Vedanta.

Vairāgya
Dispassion; renunciation.

Vajra bandha
(also known as *mūla bandha*) *See* Bandha.

Vasishtha
Ancient sage and Guru of Lord Rama. *See* Yoga Vāsishtha.

Vedanta
(lit. "end of the Vedas") One of the six orthodox schools of Indian philosophy. It arose from discussions in the Upanishads about the nature of the Absolute or the Self. *See also* Upanishads.

Vijñāna Bhairava
An exposition of the path of *yoga* based on the principles of Kashmir Shaivism. Originally composed in Sanskrit, probably in the 7th century, it describes 112 *dhāranās* or centering exercises which give the immediate experience of union with God.

Vishnu
The supreme Lord. In the Hindu trinity, the aspect of God as the sustainer of the creation. It is said that during times of wickedness and turmoil, Vishnu incarnates on the earth to protect human beings and reestablish righteousness. Rama and Krishna are among the most important of these incarnations. *See also* Brahma; Shiva.

Vishuddha
See Chakra.

Vishvamitra
A celebrated sage. As a king he visited Vasishtha's hermitage and tried to obtain the cow of plenty. His defeat was so humiliating that he undertook extreme austerities. He became a *brāhmin* and a *rishi*, and is said to be the author of nearly the entire *Rig Veda*.

Viveka
Discrimination. *See also* Vivekachūdāmani.

Vivekachūdāmani
(lit. "Crest-Jewel of Discrimination")

An 8th-century Sanskrit treatise on Advaita Vedanta by Shankaracharya. It expounds the monistic philosophy that only Brahman, the Absolute, the universal Soul, is real and that the individual soul is identical with Brahman.

Vritti
A wave or movement of the mind.

Yajña
1) A sacrificial fire ritual. Vedic *mantras* are recited as different woods, fruits, grains, oils, yogurt, and ghee are poured into the fire as an offering to the Lord, in gratitude for all we have received. 2) Any work or practice done in a spirit of sacrifice to God.

Yajñavalkya
(dates unknown) A sage whose teachings are recorded in the *Brihadāranyaka Upanishad;* the Guru of King Janaka.

Yamas
Restraints recommended for the practice of *yoga*, such as abstention from violence, falsehood, theft, and acquisitiveness. *See also* Niyamas.

Yoga
(lit. ''union'') The state of oneness with the Self, with God; the practices leading to that state. *See also* Bhakti Yoga, Hatha Yoga, Jñāna Yoga, Kundalinī Yoga, Mantra Yoga, Siddha Yoga.

Yoga Sūtras
The basic scripture of the path of *rāja yoga*, a collection of aphorisms written in Sanskrit by Patanjali, probably in the 4th century A.D. He expounds different methods for the attainment of the state of *yoga* or *samādhi*, in which the movement of the mind ceases, and the Witness rests in its own bliss. *See also* Patanjali.

Yoga Vāsishtha
(also known as *Vāsishtha-Rāmāyana)* A very popular Sanskrit text on Advaita Vedanta, probably written in the 12th century, and ascribed to the sage Valmiki. Vasishtha answers Lord Rama's philosophical questions on life, death, and human suffering. Its main teaching is that all of creation is nothing other than modifications of the mind. The world is as you see it, and when the mind is stilled, illusion ceases.

Yogi
One who practices *yoga*; also, one who has attained perfection through yogic practices. *See also* Yoga.

Zipruanna
A great Maharashtrian Siddha dearly loved by Baba Muktananda. It was Zipruanna who sent Baba to Bhagawan Nityananda.

INDEX

TO VOLUME I

Change, 41, 111, 116-117, 177
    and conviction, 130
    Truth and, 88, 112
Chanting, 2, 4, 5, 16, 106
    effects of, 2, 36, 78-79, 107
    fear and, 17-18, 44
    instructions for, 5, 44, 51, 85, 95
    of *Jay Jay Vitthal*, 74, 106
    kundalinī and, 80, 91
    of *Om*, 17, 87
    of *Om Namah Shivāya*, 17, 44, 51,
        85, 95, 121, 132, 142, 182
    in Sanskrit, 7
    See also Mantra; Sound
Children, 41
    disciplining, 150-151
    freedom of, 106
Chitta, 148
Chittam mantraha, 130
Christ. *See* Jesus
Civilization
    ego of, 67-68, 71, 72
    Japanese, 72-73
    Western, 68
Color, experience of, 137
    See also Blue Pearl; Light
Command, Guru's, 128-129, 153
Commitment, 28, 130
Company, good and bad, 79-80, 88
    and unsteadiness of mind,
        111-112
    See also Satsang
Compassion, 8, 166
Concepts. *See* Thoughts
Conceptualization, 117
    See also Thoughts
Conflict
    See also Separation
Consciousness
    all-pervasiveness of, 4, 16, 64,
        82, 84, 92, 95
    body as, 181
    and conceptualization, 117
    light of, 80-81
    perfect "I"-, 16, 17, 88
    play of, 104, 182
    pure, 16, 17, 25
    states of, 24, 25, 53

See also Experience(s); Light;
        Meditation; Siddha Yoga
Contemplation, 2, 39, 71, 72, 88, 90
    in *āshram*, 123
    of *kundalinī*, 80-81
    of lightness, 121
    See also Practices, Siddha Yoga
Contentment, 2, 27, 41, 170, 177
Conviction, firm, 130, 166, 171
Courage, 87-88
Cravings,
    See also Desire(s)

D

Darshan line, experiences and
        questions, 72, 80, 113-114, 115,
        169-170
Death, 68-69, 168-169
    fear of, 38-39, 44
    of individuality, 128
    as merging, 84
    See also Birth and death
Deception, 100, 137
Delusion, 34, 120
    veil of, 35, 100
Dervish, 177-179
Desire(s), 9, 37, 57, 100, 136, 174
    for God, 40, 124, 155
    meditation and, 136
    and Shakti, 128
    See also Attachment(s); Senses
Destiny, 104
Detachment, 38, 39-40
    of disciple, 128, 129
    in meditation, 180
Devotion, 40, 41
    three kinds of, 42
    See also Discipleship
Dharma, 101, 104
Dhyāna,
    See also Meditation
Dīkshā. See Initiation; Shaktipat
Discipleship, 104, 123-125, 171
    Bhagavad Gītā on, 145, 148, 150,
        160, 165

I

"I am that I am," 16
Ibrahim, and lost needle, 55-56
"I"-consciousness, perfect. *See*
    Pūrno aham vimarsha
Idā, 160
Identification, 44, 105
    discipleship and, 129
    false, 56
    See also Attachment(s); Ego
Ignorance, 8, 22-23, 25, 26, 33, 43
Illness, 14, 43, 79, 83-84
    See also Body; Health
Illusion, 3, 26, 36
    See also Māyā
Impurities
    See also Desire(s); Ego; *Malas;*
      Purification
Inaction, 8-9
    See also Action(s)
India, 74
Indifference, 50, 57, 169
Ingratitude, 8, 99
Initiation, 62, 77, 119
    from Swami Muktananda, 13-14
    of Sundardas, 8
    See also Shaktipat
Inner Principle. *See* Principle,
    inner
Inner Self. *See* Consciousness;
    Meditation; Self
Inspiration, 13
Intellect, 44, 70
Intensive, 175, 180
Intoxication
    divine, 2, 50, 67
    of ego, 69
Invocation, 49
Islamic thought, 14-15

J

Jālandhara bandha, 160
Janaka, King, 23-24
Japan, 1
    civilization of, 72-73
Jay Jay Vitthal, meaning of, 74,

    106-107
Jealousy, 157
    See also Māyā
Jehan, Shah, 147
Jñāna yoga, 107
Jnaneshwar Maharaj (quotations)
    on Blue Pearl, 141
    on discipleship, 149, 160, 171
    on freedom, 175, 180
    on the light of Consciousness,
      137
    on purity, 156
    on service to Guru, 153
    on world as grace, 175
Jñāneshwarī, 155
John of the Cross, Saint, 4
Joy
    of practices, 17, 36
    service and, 57, 155

K

Kabir (quotations), 5, 14, 28, 29,
    104, 126, 146, 168
    and Kamal, 126
Kamal, 126
Karma
    See also Bondage
Kashmir Shaivism, 16, 67, 85, 140
    See also Shiva Sūtras
Kathā japaha, 104
Katha Upanishad, 151
Knowledge, 35, 37, 43-44, 67, 71, 77
    fire of, 70
    See also Enlightenment; *Jñāna*
      yoga; Liberation
Koan, 5
Koran, 15
Koshas
    See also Sheaths, five
Krishna, Lord
    See also Bhagavad Gītā
Krishnasuta, 119
Kulārnava Tantra (quotations)
    on contemplation, 39
Kundalinī
    awakening of, 77, 78, 79, 80-81,
      82

and Blue Pearl, 141
and grace, 161
patience and, 170

thoughts in, 180
See also Blue Pearl; Posture(s);
   Practices, Siddha Yoga;
   Siddha Yoga
Memory, 35
Merging
   experience of, 16-17, 35, 43, 56,
      59, 84, 163, 180
   nonviolence and, 153
   service and, 57
Mexico City, 59, 67, 69, 77
Mind, 14, 70, 129, 130, 150, 151
   discipline of, 73, 115, 160
   evenness of, 10, 12, 177
   habits of, 81, 101
   purification of, 79, 92, 128
   states of, 24, 25, 118
   stillness of, 36, 52, 54, 117, 120,
      148, 160
   unsteadiness of, 110-111, 116
Mirabai (quotations), 79, 80
Miracles, 81, 83, 85, 114-115, 138,
   169
   See also Grace
Misery, 10, 14, 17, 64, 92, 110
Mistakes, 39
Moderation, 21-22, 27
Monkhood. See Sannyāsa
Motive, 9
   See also Expectations
Muktananda Paramahamsa,
      Swami (Baba), 3, 138, 173, 176,
      180
   on becoming a Guru, 123-125
   on Blue Pearl, 135, 136, 137, 138,
      140-141
   on centers of sensation, 138
   detachment of, 38, 39-40
   and discipleship, 123-125, 127,
      129, 157-158, 179-180
   on disciplining children, 150-151
   on grace, 94
   and Gurumayi, 123-124, 139-140,
      152
   on imparting teachings, 125, 129
   on *mantra*, 92
   on meditation, 5, 88, 135
   message of, 88, 111

receiving Shaktipat from, 13-14, 84
sādhanā of, 35, 49, 111, 135
and service, 153-154
and suffering of humanity, 10-12
tenderness of, 173
on trusting the Guru, 124
Mūlādhāra chakra, 160
Music, inner, 83-84, 138

N

Narada, 172-173
   on devotion, 40, 42, 43
Nasrudin, Sheik
   as banker, 11
   changes truth, 111
   refuses to tell time, 81
   smuggles donkeys, 60
Nature, 112, 174
   beauty of, 120
   lessons in, 125, 174, 180
Negativities, 1, 142
   See also Māyā
Neti neti, 115, 119
Nityananda, Bhagawan
   statue of, 158
Nivrittinath, 141
Niyamas, Yamas and, 160
Nonattachment, 167-168, 181-182
Nonchalance, 57
Nonviolence, 145, 150, 163
Nothingness, experience of, 13, 34

O

Oakland, 33, 39, 47, 80, 84
Offering, 72, 87, 104, 136, 147
Om, 16, 87
   inner reverberations of, 17
Om Namah Shivāya, 17-18, 44, 51,
      64-65, 85, 95, 121, 132, 142, 182
   syllable *ya* of, 130
   See also Chanting; *Mantra*;
      Purification; Sound
Oneness, 4, 16, 82, 84, 95
   experience of, 92, 118, 158, 182
One-pointedness, 49, 91, 142
   of Baba Muktananda, 154

patience and, 169-170
practices and, 49
process of, 123
Swami Muktananda's, 35, 49, 111, 135
Sadness, 23, 165
See also Sorrow
Sages
of Maharashtra, 74
mantra and, 104
and Nature, 125-126
See also individual sages; Saints, lessons of
Sahasrāra, 141, 161
Saints, 51, 52, 60, 83, 152
lessons of, 89-90, 100-101, 102-103, 104, 112, 116, 125, 126, 151-152, 154-155, 159, 172-173, 178-179
See also individual saints; Guru; Master; Sages
Samādhi, 154, 160, 174
Samskāras, 11
Sannyāsa, 28, 29
Gurumayi's *darshan* with Baba before, 124
Gurumayi's experience of, 152
Sanskrit, 7, 9, 87
Satsang, 79, 159
Sattva, 42
Scientists
and brain research, 78
on chanting and health, 79
and space shuttle, 41
Scriptures, 22-23
See also individual scriptures
Secret of the Siddhas (quotations), 138-139, 140-141
Self
nature of, 25-26
Swami Muktananda's message of inner, 88, 111
See also Ātman; Awakening, inner; Blue Pearl; Consciousness; Experience(s), of Self; Meditation
Self-control, 21, 22, 145, 160, 169, 171

Self-inquiry, 2, 23, 25-26, 33, 104, 107
discipleship and, 149, 150
Selfishness, 57
Self-realization, 2-3
See also Enlightenment; Experience(s), of Self; Knowledge; Liberation
Sense pleasures, 102
See also Desire(s); Ego
Senses, 50, 57, 67, 150
and awareness, 72, 81, 82, 84
centers of, 137-138
control of, 14, 91, 101, 106, 115, 117
Separation
concepts and, 14
vanishes, 16
Serenity, 2, 45, 99, 115, 169
See also Contentment; Peace
Serpent power. *See Kundalinī*
Service, 57, 64, 145, 153
Sevā, 153
Shah Jehan. *See* Jehan, Shah
Shaivism. *See* Kashmir Shaivism
Shakti, 49, 123, 140
blockage of, 128, 176
persistence and, 135
surrender and, 154, 169
Shaktipat, 13-14, 61, 85, 175
See also Awakening, inner; Initiation
Shankaracharya. *See Aparokshā-nubhūti*; *Vivekachūdāmani*
Sheik Farid. *See* Farid, Sheik
Sheik Nasrudin. *See* Nasrudin, Sheik
Shiva Purāna (quotations), 161, 162-163
Shiva Samhitā (quotation), 78
Shiva Sūtras (quotations), 104, 130, 163, 174, 175
Shrī Vidyā Antar Yāga (quotation), 80
Sickness. *See* Health
Siddha. *See* Guru; Master
Siddha Meditation, *See* Meditation; Siddha Yoga